ASTROLIT

THIS BOOK BELONGS TO:

AstroLit

AstroLit

A BIBLIOPHILE'S GUIDE
TO THE STARS

McCormick Templeman and Rachel Feder

Illustrations by Mike Willcox

CLARKSON POTTER/PUBLISHERS

New York

For Isak Sjursen—still
the grumpiest saint.

—MT

For Jed Feder and Tiffany
Tatreau, two of my favorite stars.

—RF

CONTENTS

WHY ASTROLIT?!

THIS BOOK STARTED WITH A REALLY, *REALLY* GOOD PLATE OF TOFU.

Once upon a time, two astrology buffs and literary studies scholars (that's us!) were grabbing a quick lunch and chatting about their shared teaching and research projects. Before they, er, *we* knew it, we had Percy Bysshe Shelley, Mary Shelley, and Lord Byron's charts open. We were looking at what the birth of Frankenstein's monster had to do with the stars. And let us tell you, those birth charts were *helpful.*

Here's the thing about literary studies. While novels, poetry, plays, and other literary creations are based in history, biography, and reality, they often aren't *true* per se. Even so, they can reveal deep truths about the human experience, sometimes better than straightforward truth-telling can.

In literary studies, we try to squeeze the juice out of literary artifacts. Our juice press of choice is usually a question, topic, or theory that we bring to bear on the literature in question. So we ask, how do we read *Pride & Prejudice* differently if we look at it through the lens of gender? How about through the lens of economics or real estate or storytelling style or law? Through the lens of Jane Austen's own broken engagement? (She was a total Sagittarius.)

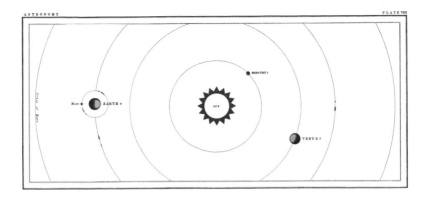

With this in mind, *AstroLit* was born from a simple question; namely, what would happen if we looked at literary history through the lens of astrology? We contend that astrology, like literature, is beautiful and useful whether or not you believe it's *true*. Like literature, astrology can spur us to action, inspire us to nurture our gifts, and encourage a deeper understanding of ourselves and others. And like literature, astrology is creative and inspiring and downright *fun*.

So, what happens when we look at literary history through the lens of astrology? You hold the answer in your hands: a book of revelations about literary figures, a guide to famous and lesser-known masterpieces, and a collection of prompts for readers, writers, and book lovers of all kinds.

We hope this little book will be an important resource for you and yours for years to come. The sky's the limit!

❋   •

YOURS WITH HEARTS AND STARS,

McCormick & Rachel ★

A REVIEW OF ASTROLOGICAL TERMS

SIGNS AND SYMBOLS

The zodiac is divided into twelve signs, and each sign is signified by a symbol and a glyph:

ARIES: *The Ram* ♈

TAURUS: *The Bull* ♉

GEMINI: *The Twins* ♊

CANCER: *The Crab* ♋

LEO: *The Lion* ♌

VIRGO: *The Maiden* ♍

LIBRA: *The Scales* ♎

SCORPIO: *The Scorpion* ♏

SAGITTARIUS: *The Archer* ♐

CAPRICORN: *The Goat* ♑

AQUARIUS: *The Water Bearer* ♒

PISCES: *The Fish* ♓

PLANETS

Each of the signs is ruled by a planet or, in some cases, two. They are as follows:

ARIES *is ruled by Mars.*

TAURUS *is ruled by Venus.*

GEMINI *is ruled by Mercury.*

CANCER *is ruled by the Moon.*

LEO *is ruled by the Sun.*

VIRGO *is ruled by Mercury.*

LIBRA *is ruled by Venus.*

SCORPIO *is ruled by Mars and Pluto.*[*]

SAGITTARIUS *is ruled by Jupiter.*

CAPRICORN *is ruled by Saturn.*

AQUARIUS *is ruled by Saturn and Uranus.*

PISCES *is ruled by Jupiter and Neptune.*

---

[*] In astrology, Pluto is recognized as a planet, although they seem to be calling it a dwarf planet these days.

ELEMENTS

Each sign is ruled by one of the four elements, giving each of the signs an associated elemental flavor. They are grouped as follows:

FIRE: *Aries, Leo, Sagittarius*

EARTH: *Taurus, Virgo, Capricorn*

AIR: *Gemini, Libra, Aquarius*

WATER: *Cancer, Scorpio, Pisces*

QUALITIES

Each of the signs is endowed with a quality or mode that speaks to the kind of energy it holds. A sign is either cardinal, fixed, or mutable. Cardinal signs are initiating and are the signs that begin each season of the year. Fixed signs are stable and unchanging and occupy the middle of a season. Mutable signs are dynamic and represent the transition from one season into the next.

CARDINAL SIGNS: *Aries, Cancer, Libra, Capricorn*

FIXED SIGNS: *Taurus, Leo, Scorpio, Aquarius*

MUTABLE SIGNS: *Gemini, Virgo, Sagittarius, Pisces*

THE TWELVE HOUSES OF THE ZODIAC

CAPRICORN · 10th
SAGITTARIUS · 9th
AQUARIUS · 11th
SCORPIO · 8th
PISCES · 12th
LIBRA · 7th
ARIES · 1st
VIRGO · 6th
TAURUS · 2nd
LEO · 5th
GEMINI · 3rd
CANCER · 4th

SUN

HOUSES

The zodiac is divided into twelve houses.

Each house deals with a different aspect of life, and although each individual's birth chart will differ in terms of which sign rules which house, there is a *natural* ruler of each house.

They are as follows:

1ST HOUSE: *Self / Aries*

2ND HOUSE: *Material wealth and prosperity / Taurus*

3RD HOUSE: *Communication, siblings, immediate environment / Gemini*

4TH HOUSE: *Home and family / Cancer*

5TH HOUSE: *Romance, creativity, and children / Leo*

6TH HOUSE: *Health and daily work / Virgo*

7TH HOUSE: *Partnership / Libra*

8TH HOUSE: *Sex, death, and other people's money / Scorpio*

9TH HOUSE: *Philosophy, higher education, and travel / Sagittarius*

10TH HOUSE: *Career / Capricorn*

11TH HOUSE: *Friends and social networks / Aquarius*

12TH HOUSE: *The Unknown / Pisces*

DETRIMENT

When a planet is positioned in the sign opposite its natural ruler, the planet is in its detriment—a sign it does not like to occupy. Think of it as a space where one is naturally uncomfortable. We say a planet is in its detriment when it falls in these signs:

THE SUN *is in its detriment in Aquarius.*

THE MOON *is in its detriment in Capricorn.*

MERCURY *is in its detriment in Sagittarius and Pisces.*

VENUS *is in its detriment in Aries and Scorpio.*

MARS *is in its detriment in Taurus and Libra.*

JUPITER *is in its detriment in Gemini and Virgo.*

SATURN *is in its detriment in Cancer and Leo.*

EXALTATION

Sometimes a planet is exalted—meaning especially well situated—in a particular sign. The exaltations are as follows:

THE SUN *is exalted in Aries.*

THE MOON *is exalted in Taurus.*

MERCURY *is exalted in Virgo.*

VENUS *is exalted in Pisces.*

MARS *is exalted in Capricorn.*

JUPITER *is exalted in Cancer.*

SATURN *is exalted in Libra.*

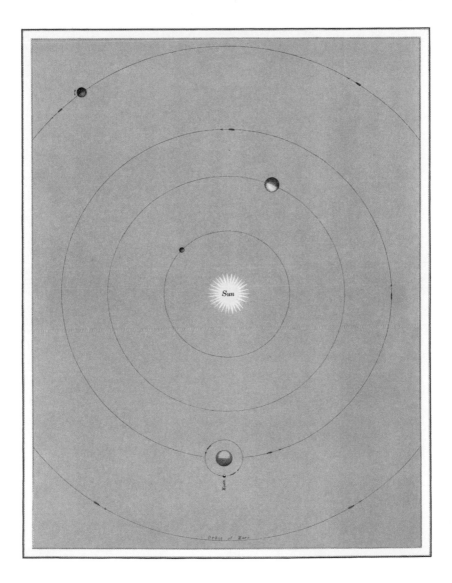

Sun

Moon

Orbit of Mars

A REVIEW OF LITERARY TERMS

ALLUSION: An indirect reference to something else.

ANAPHORA: Repeating the first word of a line.

AVANT-GARDE: Innovative for its historical period.

BALLAD: A popular narrative poem or song.

BILDUNGSROMAN: A novel focused on the formative years of its main character.

CANONICAL: Widely respected and regarded as high art.

DECADENT: Focused on the aesthetics of excess and artificiality.

DENOUEMENT: The resolution of a plot.

DOUBLE ENTENDRE: Double meaning.

DRAMATIC MONOLOGUE: Passage spoken by one character, either as part of a play or as a stand-alone poem.

EPISTLES: Letters.

EPISTOLARY: Taking the form of letters.

GENRE: A category of art with an established set of conventions and expectations. Examples include mystery, science fiction, and literary fiction.

GOTHIC: Dark, suspenseful literature, often including supernatural or seemingly supernatural specters and cavernous spaces haunted by a strange relationship to the past.

HYBRID LITERATURE: Work that combines or draws from multiple genres.

JUVENILIA: Work, often unpublished, produced when a writer (or other artist) was still young and before they developed their mature style.

POSTMODERN: Work that comes after modernism, sometimes notable for its self-aware, experimental style.

REALIST/REALISM: Literature that adheres to the depth and complexity of reality and pays attention to the systems and structures that define the lives of different people in the real world.

RHETORIC: A kind of discourse intended to persuade.

ROMANTIC/ROMANTICISM: Literature that originated in the late eighteenth and early nineteenth centuries, often marked by heightened emotions and a deep engagement with nature.

ROMAN À CLEF: A novel representing actual people or events in disguised form.

SATIRE: A work of art that relies heavily on ironic, humorous representation, usually as a means of social criticism.

SENTIMENTAL: A term used to describe eighteenth-century and later fiction focused on eliciting an emotional response from the reader.

SONNET: A fourteen-line poem, often with some sort of turn, or "volta."

SPEAKER: Conventional term used to write or talk about who is speaking in a poem without mixing that voice up with the poet. The idea of the speaker makes the most sense when discussing a poem where a character is speaking, such as a dramatic monologue.

TRANSCENDENTALIST/ TRANSCENDENTALISM: An American philosophical movement from the mid-nineteenth century that focused on the goodness of people and nature and the connections between everyday life and divine experience.

VICTORIAN: Referring to the period when Queen Victoria ruled in England, corresponding roughly with the second half of the nineteenth century (1837–1901).

+ ARIES +

ARIES

THE INCISIVE WRITER

THE CHILD IS FATHER OF THE MAN.

—William Wordsworth

ARIES 101

Aries are something of a zodiacal Rorschach test. They are what they are, and they are that thing to the extreme, but what you make of them tends to say more about you than it does about them. A cardinal fire sign, and the natural ruler of the 1st House, Aries starts the zodiac out with a bang. The 1st House is the house of the self. It is the realm of personal power, calculated trajectory, and self-focus. It's no surprise, then, that Aries can sometimes err on the side of egotism.

As the first of the twelve signs, Aries are the originators of the zodiac. They create the path that the rest of us walk, but they can sometimes be a little aggressive about telling us how to walk it. They are also associated with youth and with a potentially harmful refusal to grow up. That same youthful enthusiasm that helps them move mountains and inspires the rest of us to follow them with awed devotion can twist into bratty self-centeredness if they're not careful.

Symbolized by the ram, Aries surge out into the world with temerity and courage. They confront every issue head-on, horns forward, and ready to take on any foe they might meet along the path. Ruled by Mars, Aries is the sign in which the Sun is exalted. That's a lot of fire for one sign. As the god of war in ancient Roman mythology, Mars is a figure of hostility and conflict, but his aggression is not without a purpose. The warlike nature of Mars is not grounded in chaos or evil, but intended

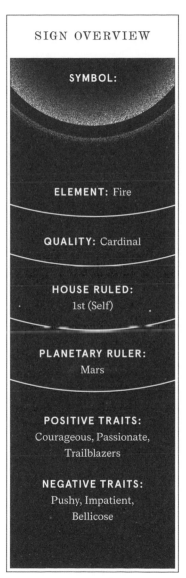

SIGN OVERVIEW

SYMBOL:

ELEMENT: Fire

QUALITY: Cardinal

HOUSE RULED:
1st (Self)

PLANETARY RULER:
Mars

POSITIVE TRAITS:
Courageous, Passionate,
Trailblazers

NEGATIVE TRAITS:
Pushy, Impatient,
Bellicose

to be a means of achieving and maintaining peace. Similarly, Aries believe that the best defense is a good offense, and though it may seem like they are just fighting to fight, they are actually impelled by a strong sense of justice and a desire to right any wrongs . . . before they even occur.

While Mars gives Aries its bellicose side, the Sun gives Aries an infectious, almost raging enthusiasm that either draws you to them or scares you away in an instant. Either way, the path for an Aries tends to open up in front of them no matter which direction they decide to go. And they may decide to change direction at any time. They thrive on conflict, but they don't like to lose. Nor do they like to be questioned. Well, maybe they like it just a little bit if it promises to lead to a good fight, but not if it diminishes their sense of self or restricts them in any way. Freedom-loving to the extreme, Aries simply must be allowed to go where they want and do what they desire, and woe be it to any and all who try to stand in their way.

THE ARIES WRITER:
A LITERARY HISTORY

Idealistic, determined, and enigmatic, Aries writers push society forward. Their work has the potential to create breakthroughs of all kinds. Nella Larsen was an artistic trailblazer, William Wordsworth redefined poetry for the people and journeyed inward to craft a philosophy of the self, Henry Derozio inspired a movement in a moment, and Anne Lister had a gay marriage in the nineteenth century by the sheer force of her will.

CASE STUDY #1: NELLA LARSEN

As the first sign of the zodiac, Aries like to start out big, they like to win, and more often than not, they are first to cross a finish line. Such is the case with Nella Larsen, born on April 13, 1891, to Mary Hanson Walker, a white Danish immigrant, and Peter Walker, a West Indian cook most likely of Afro-Caribbean descent. Larsen's father died when she was only two, and her mother went on to marry Peter Larsen, a Danish immigrant, who adopted Nella.

After finishing high school, Larsen attended Fisk University followed by nursing school. Larsen excelled in the field and quickly rose to the top of her class, but she wouldn't stick with nursing. Instead, she married Dr. Elmer Imes (Libra), a physics professor (and the second Black person to receive a PhD in physics), and the two made a home for themselves among the Black academic class in New York City. While living in New York, Larsen was very involved in her community and volunteered at the public library. There she met Ernestine Rose (Pisces), a feminist librarian with strong ties to many Harlem Renaissance artists. With Rose's encouragement, Larsen attended Columbia's New York Public Library School and became the first Black woman to earn a degree from the institution (remember, Aries have a tendency to do things first).

Degree in hand, Larsen set to work as a librarian, serving in a branch on the Lower East Side of Manhattan, but she soon transferred to the Harlem branch where she became interested in the work of local Harlem Renaissance artists. Initially, Larsen dwelled on the periphery of the Renaissance, but she would go on to find her place at the center of the movement and would be remembered as one of its most prominent literary talents. She counted Dorothy Randolph Peterson (Gemini-Cancer cusp, see "A Note on Cusp Figures," page 274), Walter White (Cancer), Carl Van Vechten (Gemini), and Jessie Redmon Fauset (Taurus, see page 54) among her close friends.

Larsen published her first story in 1926, followed by her first novel, *Quicksand* (1928), a roman à clef about a young woman of mixed race who travels the world in an effort to come to terms with her own unexamined prejudices. *Quicksand* was very well received, but it was Larsen's second novel, *Passing* (1929), that would secure her a place among the literati. Upon its publication, *Passing* was a critical and commercial success, and after a quiet spell, it eventually surged into the literary canon. Focused on two women of mixed race, Irene and Clare, the latter of whom chooses to pass for white while the former settles contentedly into her upper-middle-class Black existence, *Passing* is about systemic racism, internalized prejudice, and colorism, but it is also a deeply compelling psychological suspense novel. Composed in a tense, electric style, *Passing* is in many ways a progenitor of novels like *Gone Girl* and *The Girl on the Train*. One could even argue that Patricia Highsmith (Capricorn) might be thematically indebted to Larsen. As much as *Passing* is about race and class, it is also an extremely adept meditation on female friendship, homosocial desire, and the fascination one woman can have for a certain type of dangerous woman she sees as her antithetical double. In Irene, Clare sees the life she left behind and for which she deeply longs—a life she will gamble everything she holds dear to get a taste of once again. Conversely, in Clare,

Irene sees everything she is not—a daredevil, a temptress, and even a race traitor—and the intense fascination the two women hold for each other makes for a wildly addictive read. While dealing thoughtfully with deeply troubling questions of bigotry and injustice, Larsen also manages to take the reader on a high-speed journey of paranoia, sexual jealousy, and, ultimately, violence. We won't spoil the end for you, but let's just say it will stay with you.

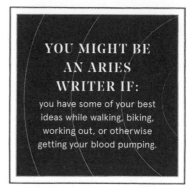

YOU MIGHT BE AN ARIES WRITER IF: you have some of your best ideas while walking, biking, working out, or otherwise getting your blood pumping.

Larsen went on to win a Guggenheim Fellowship—the first Black woman ever to do so—but she wouldn't stay long in the literary world. Aries seldom stick around after conquering a dream or passion. New vistas tend to call, and Aries rams find mountains that insist on being summitted. After a divorce and a plagiarism scandal (of which she was ultimately cleared), Larsen abruptly disappeared from Harlem's soirées and literary salons, and she never published again.

Aries writers have a way of causing as much of a stir as the larger-than-life characters they create, and Larsen was no exception. After her departure from the literary scene, rumors abounded that she herself had "passed," disappearing into the vast quagmire of white society. However, the truth is much less mysterious. In reality, she never even left New York. She simply moved downtown and resumed her nursing career.

Aries can get a bad rap as a sign perpetually determined to be the center of attention, but there is often a very real valor and heroism that courses through their veins. They are the warriors and the heroes of the zodiac, and sometimes heroes don't stick around to lap up their literary glory in the soft glow of their Guggenheims. Sometimes they roll up their sleeves and get to work, nursing the sick without so much as a drop of public attention.

CASE STUDY #2: WILLIAM WORDSWORTH

It's hard to imagine a better name for an Aries writer than "Wordsworth." Often doggedly committed to a higher cause, or many causes, the Aries writer knows that their words are worth much more than it might appear. At the same time, Aries writers might overidentify their self-worth with their creative output, leading them to produce an overwhelming amount of text or to overedit an inspired idea into oblivion. All these things were true of the great English poet William Wordsworth, an author who was such a stereotypical Aries, he often wrote while walking.

William Wordsworth was born in Cumberland, England, in 1770, the second of five children. His sister, Dorothy Wordsworth (Sagittarius, see page 205), who would become a major figure in his life, was born the following year, but the two were soon separated. Following the death of Wordsworth's mother in 1778, he was sent to Hawkshead Grammar School, where visitors can still see his name carved into his desk. Notably, the Lake District village of Hawkshead was later home to the children's author Beatrix Potter (Leo); if you picture the quaint setting of *The Tale of Peter Rabbit*, you'll get a pretty good sense of the surroundings. Around this time, Dorothy Wordsworth was sent to live with their grandparents. The two siblings would not be reunited until 1794, when they were in their early twenties. Their father also passed away when they were young, and their adulthood was marked by collaborative experiments in home and family making, experiments that exemplify the Aries alchemy that can turn everything from quotidian tasks to past trauma into new projects.

The sky rejoices in the morning's birth.

—WILLIAM WORDSWORTH

Wordsworth began attending college and publishing poems. In 1790, while on a walking tour in France with a friend, he found himself inspired by the celebrations of the first anniversary of the French Revolution. He returned to France the following year, where he spent time with an army officer, Michel de Beaupuy (Cancer), an influential friend who educated him about the politics of the revolution. While in France, Wordsworth also fell in love with another Cancer, Annette Vallon, with whom he fathered a child, Anne-Caroline (Sagittarius). But Wordsworth had likely already left France by the time Anne-Caroline was born, and the outbreak of war between France and England kept him from returning until much later.

Reunited with Dorothy in England, Wordsworth mixed with radical circles, including those involved with the radical press in London. Eventually, he settled in beautiful Alfoxden near his major collaborator and lifelong frenemy, Samuel Taylor Coleridge (Libra, see page 164). At this point, England had started to crack down on radicals and had passed a series of acts criminalizing public assemblies and speeches critical of the government. Rumors circulated that Wordsworth and Coleridge were French spies and they became subject to surveillance by the authorities. This ordeal is sometimes called the "Spy Nosy" affair, since one eavesdropper misheard Wordsworth and Coleridge discussing the philosopher Baruch Spinoza (Sagittarius) and thought they were talking about being "spy-nosy." Eager to commit to higher causes, whether political, social, or intellectual, an Aries won't always watch their words or think about how an audience might interpret what they hear. When it comes to writing, this means that revision can be their friend—although, as we'll see with Wordsworth, it can also be their foe.

In 1798, Wordsworth and Coleridge published the first edition of their collaborative masterwork, *Lyrical Ballads*. The book was highly experimental, blending the literary techniques of high poetry with the folksier elements of the ballad tradition in order to cut to the core of the intersecting crises plaguing folks in rural England. Sons and husbands had gone off to war against France, the industrial revolution was causing the death of cottage industries, and the privatization and enclosure of what had been communal lands hurt farmers and laborers. The combination of these sociopolitical forces strained the rural poor and led to hunger, poverty, and tragedy. In his contributions to *Lyrical Ballads*, Wordsworth tapped into his Aries idealism and heightened sense of injustice to capture these hardships and elevate them to high art. But incisive writing can also be violent. In many of his poems, Wordsworth included a know-it-all, mansplaining narrator who witnesses hardship without helping, acts unthoughtfully, or, in one case, even argues with a child about how she makes sense of her siblings' deaths. But is this unpleasant narrator a surrogate for the poet himself or simply a poetic device? Asserting his intellectual authority, asking often inappropriate questions, and sometimes hurting when he tries to help, Wordsworth's narrator—or narrators—can be understood as embodying some negative Aries stereotypes. At the same time, Wordsworth's masterful use of the narrator figure to highlight privilege, injustice, and societal ills speaks to the broad-based social consciousness that is the mark of the Aries writer.

The Peace of Amiens allowed Wordsworth to visit Annette and Anne-Caroline in France in 1802. He arranged for child-support payments and then returned to England and married his childhood friend Mary Hutchinson. In other words, in typical Aries fashion, he did the right thing, as long as you don't take anything personally. Dorothy continued to live with William and Mary following their marriage; they were joined by Mary's sister, Sara, with whom Coleridge fell in love. William and Mary had five children in all. The growing family made a home in the Lake District, first at tiny, industrious Dove Cottage, then at a larger home on the hillside, and finally at the stately family home of Rydal Mount. Hardy and hardworking, Wordsworth had immense poetic output all his life, and he lived well into the Victorian period, becoming Poet Laureate of England at the age of seventy-three. As he grew older, and more successful, Wordsworth

YOU MIGHT
BE AN ARIES
WRITER IF:
you tend to revise your
work into oblivion.

lost sight of his earlier radicalism, which probably has more to do with his Virgo Moon / Scorpio rising combination than with his Aries Sun, as Aries' disinterested idealism often allows for the coexistence of progressive beliefs and normative success.

No discussion of the Aries writer would be complete without mentioning two Wordsworth poems in particular: his masterpiece and the poem he never wrote. The masterpiece is Wordsworth's poetic autobiography, *The Prelude*, in which he chronicled the "growth of a poet's mind" through his childhood spent in nature to his defining education, reading, and travels. *The Prelude* is a deep journey inward, one that dwells not only on the sublime vistas seen from mountaintops but also on the limitless depths of the human soul. Wordsworth finished the first version of *The Prelude* in 1805, but he continued to revise it for the rest of his life, and it was published only posthumously in 1850. However, Wordsworth would likely be frustrated to know that scholars generally agree that the 1805 version is the best and that forty-five years of revision only made the poem worse.

While he was tinkering with *The Prelude*, Wordsworth *wasn't* finishing his great philosophical poem, *The Recluse*. In fact, Wordsworth claimed *The Prelude* was the introduction to *The Recluse*, a sort of antechamber to the Gothic cathedral of his great work. But the work Wordsworth put into *The Recluse* never lived up to the idea in his mind, so he procrastinated by continuing to revise *The Prelude*. Thus, while Wordsworth was ultimately one of the most successful, prolific, and influential poets in the English tradition, his story also holds two important warnings to the Aries writer: sometimes it's time to let the work be done, and nobody can read the book you keep in your head.

CRUSH-WORTHY MEN

according to *Frankenstein* author Mary Shelley (Virgo)

1. **PERCY BYSSHE SHELLEY** (Leo), the Romantic poet she "eloped" with even though he was married to somebody else

2. **WASHINGTON IRVING** (Aries), the first American writer to gain international renown

3. **PROSPER MÉRIMÉE (KINDA)** (Libra), a French author best remembered for his novella *Carmen*, which inspired the opera of the same name

4. **AUBREY BEAUCLERK** (another Leo), a radical politician

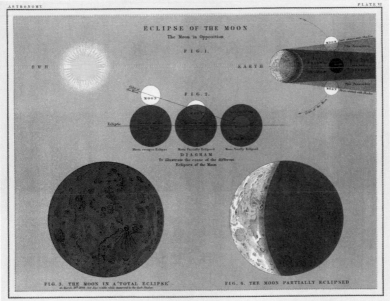

CASE STUDY #3: HENRY DEROZIO

Although Anglo-Indian poet Henry Derozio lived a tragically short life, his influences—and his influence—were great. Born in Kolkata on April 18, 1809, to an Indian father and an English mother, he received a liberal education among children from different social classes and national backgrounds. As a student, he read British Romantic poetry by his contemporaries John Keats (Scorpio, see page 175), Percy Bysshe Shelley (Leo, see page 106), and Lord Byron (Aquarius, see "A Note on Cusp Figures," page 274), and found himself inspired by the intense emotions of their work. A move in his early teens to Bhagalpur, where Derozio worked in his uncle's indigo factory, added to these literary inspirations the sweeping, scenic views around the Ganges River. Derozio began writing and publishing poetry of his own, creating his own form of Indian Romanticism. Scholar Zeeshan Reshamwala sees an "Aries-like, playful audacity" in Derozio's work, "extending the geographical ambit of Romantic poetry."

A palanquin, illustrated for the *Official Descriptive and Illustrated Catalogue* for the Great Exhibition of the Works of Industry of All Nations, 1851.

In an early poem, Derozio imagines Byron's Don Juan (pronounced "Joo-an"), a naïve young man who can't help but seduce people wherever he goes, trying to board a palanquin in Kolkata: "Go in—but how? legs foremost, or a straddle?" Don Juan eventually needs to be shoved in.

A poem aptly titled "Poetry," which Derozio wrote when he was eighteen, captures the experience of embarking on a writerly life:

Sweet madness!—when the youthful brain is seized
With that delicious phrenzy which it loves,
It raving reels, to very rapture pleased,
—And then through all creation wildly roves

The poem goes on to list the places through which the poetry-seized mind roves, including the "highest Himalay" alongside "classic Greece," and to mention standard tropes of British Romanticism including the nightingale (often used as a symbol of the poet) and the "wilderness of ruins" that might lead the poet to contemplate death, humanity, infinity, and the very nature of time. In other words, the Romantic poets were, in general, very extra, and while Derozio wasn't palling around with Byron, Shelley, and Keats, he was certainly extra enough for their company. Derozio's ability to create his own version of British Romanticism in India speaks to the Aries talent for turning inspiration into something tangible. Although Aries can be quite countercultural, they also crave a sense of belonging and inclusion in a group, and so social, political, and artistic movements that speak to their ideals can spark intense devotion and loyalty.

This was certainly the case for Derozio, who began teaching literature and history at seventeen and soon found himself surrounded by adoring students. Coalescing around Derozio's charismatic presence and gift for cultivating conversation, students engaged in intense intellectual debates, eventually founding an official group called the Academic Association. Driven by their intense idealism and love of community, outgoing Aries like Henry Derozio are adept at starting discussion groups, societies, and book clubs, and at planning events of all sorts, making others feel welcome. Such activities speak to their highest callings. In a poem addressed to his students, Derozio wrote, "Expanding like the petals of young flowers / I watch the gentle opening of your minds." The poem concludes, "Ah then I feel I have not lived in vain."

Derozio praised the effects of wine in his poetry, a countercultural move that gave his followers a reputation for being notorious imbibers of alcohol. Aries like what they like and aren't always great at keeping their personal faves to themselves.

Sadly, Derozio received backlash from some of his students' more conservative parents; he was dismissed from his post shortly before his early death from cholera at the age of twenty-two. But Derozio's influence was felt long after this tragedy, as his students continued to make waves. Sometimes known as Derozians, sometimes called the Young Bengal Movement, a number of Derozio's former acolytes played important roles in the intellectual, social, and cultural development of their region. Such are the lingering gifts of a devoted Aries teacher.

CODA: ANNE LISTER

Anne Lister, or "Gentleman Jack," as she was sometimes called, was a prolific diarist, estate owner, and traveler based in Halifax, West Yorkshire. One of six children without much family wealth or an expected inheritance of her own, Lister would go on to become an experienced businesswoman and adventurer. Often referred to as the first modern lesbian, she left detailed records of her romantic and sexual experiences in coded portions of her four-million-word diary. Her eventual partnership was also an early and groundbreaking example of same-sex marriage in England.

Anne Lister was born on April 3, 1791. Her older brother had inherited the sprawling family estate of Shibden Hall, a property that produced enough money to live on but otherwise didn't provide the family with much disposable income. At boarding school, Lister shared an attic room nicknamed "the slope" with a biracial heiress, Eliza Raine, who became her first love. The daughter of an Indian mother and an English father, Eliza was adept with languages, and together she and Lister developed a secret code that combined Latin and Greek letters with mathematical and zodiac symbols. While at first

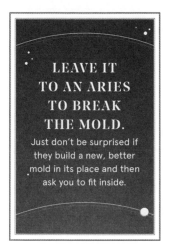

LEAVE IT
TO AN ARIES
TO BREAK
THE MOLD.
Just don't be surprised if
they build a new, better
mold in its place and then
ask you to fit inside.

this code was designed to facilitate love notes between the two schoolgirls, Lister would later use the code to privatize the portions of her diary dealing, in explicit detail, with her romantic and sexual encounters. Aries writers are nothing if not original and industrious. They also tend to tell it like it is.

After six months, Lister and her roommate had exchanged rings and promised to build a life together after leaving school. But the course of their young love didn't run smoothly. When their relationship was discovered, Lister was forced to return home until Eliza had left the school. Although the pair continued to correspond and Eliza visited Lister on her school breaks, Lister was beginning to build a life and an identity that left little room for youthful promises. She told Eliza she wanted to postpone moving in together, a delay that became permanent after four of Lister's siblings died, bringing her closer to inheriting her family's estate. A series of tragic events in Eliza's family made her a less eligible, or honorable, match for the woman who was likely to end up running Shibden Hall.

Paradoxically, Lister was interested in a bride who would bring honor to her family name even though same-sex marriage was not legalized, male homosexuality was itself illegal, and romantic love between women had no place in the public sphere. Defying gender norms in her dress and habits, Lister flirted with an unmarried woman to whom she was teaching the flute and even caused a small scandal after visiting a captain's private chambers to view his pistols. Lister was also socially and sexually involved with two young women from school, Isabella Norcliffe and Mariana Belcombe, and it's likely their opinions were

Anne wrote in her diary about being sketched for a portrait. This painting by Joshua Horner is on display at Shibden Hall.

particularly important to her. While an Aries lives by their own code and does not hesitate to defy convention, they can still get caught up in the opinions of others, codifying what were at first radical breaks from convention and becoming set in their ways.

As Eliza approached the age of her inheritance and found herself faced with a male suitor, she reached out to Lister for reassurance that the two would end up together. Instead of keeping her commitment to Eliza, Lister shared a distorted version of events with Eliza's suitor as well as with Eliza's guardian. This act of betrayal harmed Eliza's reputation and broke her heart; she would never recover. Abandoned by her beloved, plagued by sorrows in her family, and haunted by an engagement that had fallen through, Eliza was committed to an asylum. Lister visited her from time to time until Eliza's death. Though Aries are capable of deep and abiding commitment, they can also fall prey to the impulse to push others away.

In 1816, Lister suffered a heartbreak of her own when Mariana Belcombe got married. The two women continued their affair in secret, and Lister even stayed with the married couple until Mariana's husband kicked her out.

When she finally inherited her family estate, Lister applied herself to improving and running Shibden Hall. Dressed in no-nonsense black frocks, departing on frequent trips, and keeping her diary in meticulous bound volumes, Lister redefined successful femininity for herself. Her improvements to her inherited property included some classic Aries touches, such as a wilderness garden to support her love of walking.

Lister became involved with Ann Walker (Taurus), an heiress, and the two lived as a married couple until Lister's death. The pair managed to have a wedding of sorts, exchanging rings and taking communion together with the blessing of the church. Walker's funds supported Lister's entrepreneurial endeavors, including sinking coal pits on her property and opening a casino, and the couple took a series of adventurous trips together. An accomplished mountaineer and a classic Aries bighorn sheep, Lister became the first woman to ascend Mount Perdu in the Pyrenees and the first person of any gender to ascend Mount Vignemale. She died of an illness during a journey through the Caucasus at the age of forty-nine, leaving Walker to embark on a six-month journey home with her embalmed body. Put another way, Anne Lister was such a classic Aries, she kept moving even after her death.

TOTAL ECLIPSE of the SUN.

NOTES FOR WRITERS WITH OTHER ARIES PLACEMENTS

WRITER'S CORNER

POSITIVE ASPECTS

You generate new text smoothly and easily, bring boundless energy to any project, and can accomplish what you set out to do.

NEGATIVE ASPECTS

You may fall prey to perfectionism and a tendency to over-revise.

WRITER BEWARE

Your writing will never live up to the ideal in your head; better to share your best than to avoid your audience completely.

ARIES MOON: You have a drive to achieve at the very center of your being. A fiery leader to the core, you are the one to set armies marching and victory flags flying. You don't like to be told that you can't do something, and you not only demand to be the person to catalyze massive change, but also, you are often the first to do something.

ARIES RISING: You are driven by a call to adventure and have an infectious enthusiasm that gives your work a visceral and immediate attractiveness. You confront obstacles in your work that might make a different writer run for cover. In fact, you might even crave those obstacles because you thrive on conflict. Your work might be all the better for it. However, you may have a tendency to rush; slow down a tad and make sure you're not getting ahead of yourself. We also recommend a solid proofread.

MERCURY IN ARIES: You have a gift for satire and are really a tremendous wit. You can be a tad cutting with your words, but you see the world just a little bit differently than the rest of us do. Use that gift to tell us what we don't know.

VENUS IN ARIES: You live at the intersection of sensuality and aggression. This can make for some fairly interesting and potentially explosive prose. Try composing a sonnet about someone who makes you angry. Write a war story that is about love at its core. You would also do well to perform your work. You can be entrancing in your displays of literary passion.

MARS IN ARIES: You most likely don't need us to tell you how great you are and just how boundless your potential is. Your very being is infused with the confidence that you can and will accomplish whatever you set your mind to. If there is a weakness to this position, it is a tendency toward bluntness that can be off-putting. We recommend having a trusted reader look over your work before submission to make sure you're not going to ruffle any feathers you don't intend to ruffle.

TRY THIS!

+ DICTATE the first pages of a new project on a walk.

+ KEEP a daily diary and then mine it for inspiration.

+ SET a timer for fifteen minutes. During this time, keep your pen moving and try to write a biography of your mind. What influences, experiences, and relationships have shaped the way you think? What does your mind want you to put out into the world? This free-write can even take the form of a question-and-answer session. What would it look like if you could interview your own mind?

READER'S CORNER

COMPATIBILITY CHART

Which Aries-composed book is most likely to appeal to you? It depends on your sign. Look for your match below. And don't forget to look at your rising and Moon signs if you know those.

SIGN	CLASSIC	MODERN
ARIES	MAYA ANGELOU, *I Know Why the Caged Bird Sings*	JON KRAKAUER, *Into Thin Air*
TAURUS	WASHINGTON IRVING, *The Sketch-Book of Geoffrey Crayon, Gent.*	DOROTHEA LASKY, *Milk*
GEMINI	NELLA LARSEN, *Passing*	JESMYN WARD, *Sing, Unburied, Sing*
CANCER	HANS CHRISTIAN ANDERSEN, *Complete Fairy Tales*	MARY BERRY, *Recipe for Life*
LEO	WILLIAM WORDSWORTH, *The Prelude*	YOKO TAWADA, *Memoirs of a Polar Bear*
VIRGO	HENRY JAMES, *What Maisie Knew*	ILYA KAMINSKY, *Deaf Republic*

SIGN	CLASSIC	MODERN
LIBRA	HENRY DEROZIO, *The Fakeer of Jungheera: A Metrical Tale*	PAUL KALANITHI, *When Breath Becomes Air*
SCORPIO	TENNESSEE WILLIAMS, *A Streetcar Named Desire*	JERICHO BROWN, *The Tradition*
SAGITTARIUS	ROBERT FROST, *A Further Range*	PAUL THEROUX, *Figures in a Landscape*
CAPRICORN	SAMUEL BECKETT, *Krapp's Last Tape*	ADA LIMÓN, *The Hurting Kind*
AQUARIUS	FRANK O'HARA, *Lunch Poems*	BARBARA KINGSOLVER, *Prodigal Summer*
PISCES	CHARLES BAUDELAIRE, *The Flowers of Evil*	TRACY K. SMITH, *Life on Mars*

✦ TAURUS ✦

TAURUS

THE STABLE GOTH WRITER

I AM NO BIRD; AND NO NET ENSNARES ME;
I AM A FREE HUMAN BEING WITH AN INDEPENDENT WILL.

—Charlotte Brontë

TAURUS 101

Chances are you have a Taurus in your life who serves as something of a stabilizing anchor to those around them—whether that anchor is emotional, psychological, or material. These weighty aesthetes are notorious for their steadfast nature and placid demeanor, but there is much more to the sign than meets the eye. That placidity, while not exactly false, is something of a smoke screen. Tauruses are working constantly, just down below the surface where no one else can see.

A fixed earth sign, Taurus is the sign of the bull. It is from the bull that Tauruses receive their reputation for being stubborn. And we're not exactly going to argue with that assessment; we're simply going to suggest that a more accurate term might be *determined*. Yes, it's difficult to get a bull to move, but that's from your point of view. From your perspective, the bull is stubborn because it's not doing what you want, but in fact the bull is simply *determined* to do exactly as it pleases. There's quite a difference.

Venus rules Taurus, and the Moon is exalted (in its strength) in this sign. This lunar goddess energy imbues the sign with both a natural beauty and a love of all things Venusian. Tauruses appreciate luxury and comfort, and they are more than willing to work for it. They don't expect anything to be given to them; the reward of luxury and abundance is made all the sweeter by a bull's knowledge that it stems from the effort

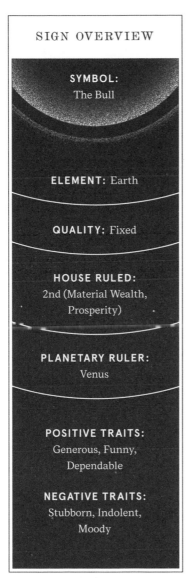

SIGN OVERVIEW

SYMBOL:
The Bull

ELEMENT: Earth

QUALITY: Fixed

HOUSE RULED:
2nd (Material Wealth,
Prosperity)

PLANETARY RULER:
Venus

POSITIVE TRAITS:
Generous, Funny,
Dependable

NEGATIVE TRAITS:
Stubborn, Indolent,
Moody

they put in under the surface and just out of sight. Due to Venus's rulership, Tauruses love their partners and families with a grounded solidity that is perhaps unmatched. They also are inclined toward an appreciation of sensuality, and it is this collision of Venus and the bull that endows Tauruses with their legendary epicureanism. Tauruses tend to be excellent cooks, and if they aren't, then at the very least they have one excellent cook in their life whom they appreciate dearly. Bulls are serious creatures. They must be fed, but because Venus presides over every aspect of this sign, that food must be not only of the highest quality, but also a thing of beauty. No kibble will suffice—break out the caviar and the poached salmon, please.

Taurus's appreciation of the finer things in life sometimes seems at odds with their famous grounded earthiness, but when one considers that Taurus is the natural ruler of the 2nd House of material wealth and prosperity, a clearer picture forms. As opposed to the 8th House, which represents the money you receive from others, the 2nd House represents the money you earn yourself, usually with the help of Taurean hard work and determination. The 2nd House rules the coming and going of worldly success and physical abundance. Because this is the natural home of Taurus, it makes sense that these grounded bulls should go in search of financial stability, filling their coffers, firming up their foundations, and perhaps tossing a feathery throw pillow onto the velvet divan. Don't fault them for it. They're simply doing their job. And while they seem to spend most of their time in that luxurious sitting room, lounging in placid tranquility, perhaps enjoying a bonbon or two, Taurus is always at work. You simply have no idea that it's happening.

THE TAURUS WRITER:
A LITERARY HISTORY

With steady hands, loving hearts, and an indomitable stubbornness, er, *determination*, Taurus writers pull intellectual and literary history forward. Sharing a Sun sign with heavyweights ranging from William Shakespeare to Karl Marx, Taurus writers draw energy and strength from their personal connections and never give up on the projects and people they care most about. Mary Wollstonecraft overcame immense hardship to found modern feminism out of love for her sisters, friends, and daughters. Charlotte Brontë turned the darkness of her life into an immortal literary legacy for her family. J. M. Barrie turned his greatest loss into a gift for generations of children, and Jessie Redmon Fauset helped create an artistic renaissance.

CASE STUDY #1: MARY WOLLSTONECRAFT

Mary Wollstonecraft was, in today's terminology, a bad bitch. Often considered to be the foremother of modern feminism, Wollstonecraft showed us that you can change the world while staying messy and a little (or a lot) *extra*. Emotional, countercultural, indefatigable, and somehow both rebellious and pragmatic, Wollstonecraft was a Taurus genius for the ages.

Born in London on April 27, 1759, Mary Wollstonecraft was the second of seven children. She had a tumultuous childhood: her father moved the family from place to place in pursuit of his professional ambitions, then descended into violent alcoholism and squandered the family's money. It became clear early on that Mary would need to make her own way in the world.

YOU MIGHT BE A TAURUS IF: you're reading this book while enjoying at least three other things that make you feel cozy: a soft blanket, a cup of tea, a slice of cake, and the new Adele album (yes, she's a Taurus, obviously!).

Throughout her youth, Wollstonecraft formed several deep and influential friendships. Perhaps most notable among these was her friendship with Fanny Blood, whom Wollstonecraft met through mutual friends at the age of sixteen. Wollstonecraft's future husband, the political theorist and writer William Godwin (Pisces), would later say she had "contracted a friendship so fervent, as for years to have constituted the ruling passion of her mind." An illustrator and educator, Fanny would later join Wollstonecraft and her sisters in founding a school. Wollstonecraft would sail to Lisbon to assist her friend in childbirth; after Fanny died giving birth, Wollstonecraft both modeled a character after her in her novella *Mary, A Fiction* and named her first daughter Fanny. Tauruses are nothing if not loyal and devoted friends, a quality that can enrich their creative projects through inspiration, collaboration, and tribute.

Following her mother's death in 1782, Wollstonecraft took responsibility for her younger siblings' futures (she had an older brother, but he wasn't on top of things). She helped her sister Eliza, who was suffering from severe postpartum depression, leave her husband and child; the child died later that year. While leaving the baby behind with a father who Wollstonecraft thought treated her sister poorly stands in stark contrast to Wollstonecraft's approach to motherhood in her political philosophy, it's important to remember that, in this period in England, it was nearly impossible for a woman to leave her husband and take custody of her child without severe social and legal backlash. In Wollstonecraft's unfinished Gothic novel, *The Wrongs of Woman, or Maria*, a mother who attempts this finds herself separated from her daughter and imprisoned in a private asylum.

With her sisters and Fanny Blood, Wollstonecraft founded the aforementioned school for girls, first at Islington and then at Newington Green. The school failed when Wollstonecraft left to assist Fanny in childbirth, after which she moved to Ireland to become a governess before returning to London to pursue a career in publishing.

Wollstonecraft's productivity intensified around this time, and she published some of her most groundbreaking social critiques and political philosophy, including *Thoughts on the Education of Daughters*, *A Vindication of the Rights of Men*, and *A Vindication of the Rights of Woman*. While she is most famous for *Rights of Woman* and this vindication is often held up as the paradigmatic text of early feminism, Wollstonecraft's political writings, though brilliant, entered into an existing, predominantly male discourse and thus didn't contain her most radical ideas. In these vindications, Wollstonecraft argues for pragmatic, systemic shifts that would lend a greater sense of justice, fairness, humility, kindness, and ethics to the patriarchal status quo in England.

Later, in her unfinished Gothic novel, Wollstonecraft would critique the patriarchal structures her political philosophy sought to reform. Though dark, twisted tales were almost universally popular in Wollstonecraft's day, the Gothic genre was seen as feminine and largely geared toward women, and often featured a heroine in distress. In *The Wrongs of Woman*, on which Wollstonecraft would still be working when she died from complications sustained in childbirth, she explored the intersections of economic, legal, and gender oppression, tackling topics including abortion, abuse, and neglect. Political philosophy was largely geared toward a male audience; Wollstonecraft was likely experimenting with Gothic fiction in order to get her ideas in front of women readers. Wollstonecraft's husband would edit and publish this novel following Wollstonecraft's death, and it would haunt her daughter, the future Mary Shelley (Virgo, see page 131), all her life.

YOU MIGHT BE
A TAURUS IF:
you're the backbone of every group text.

Through her publications and publisher, Wollstonecraft became involved in a circle of writers, artists, and radical thinkers including William Blake (Sagittarius, see page 195) and Henry Fuseli (Aquarius), an artist whose dark genius pulled her in so thoroughly, she offered to live with Fuseli and his wife in a polyamorous relationship. When they rejected her, Wollstonecraft moved to Paris, where she met American businessman Gilbert Imlay (another Aquarius). Their relationship would be intense and emotionally taxing for Wollstonecraft—after she gave birth to their daughter, Fanny Imlay, she suffered from postpartum depression, discovered her husband's infidelity, and attempted suicide twice. During this period, Wollstonecraft traveled with little Fanny to Scandinavia to assist in one of Imlay's business ventures. While her actual letters to Imlay from this period are devastating, Wollstonecraft also wrote and published a gorgeous travelogue, *Letters Written During a Short Residence in Sweden, Norway, and Denmark*. This luscious account of her travels caught the attention of her passing acquaintance William Godwin and made him fall in love with her.

We should note here that while Wollstonecraft had the Sun, Moon, Mercury, and her Midheaven (the placement most indicative of career path) in Taurus in the 9th House of education, travel, publishing, and philosophy, an astrological signature that defined her life and legacy, she was also a Virgo rising. So, she could make it look like she was having the aesthetically decadent vacation of the century even when she was really looking for lost silver and writing scathing missives to her unfaithful lover in which she threatened to throw herself into the sea. The *actual* Virgo rising up in Wollstonecraft's life was world-historical genius Mary Wollstonecraft Godwin, later Shelley, who would prove a careful and capacious acolyte of her mother's work.

Wollstonecraft left Imlay and took up with Godwin; upon discovering they were pregnant, the couple decided to wed in spite of their unconventional politics. But their marriage of the minds was cut tragically short after Wollstonecraft died from complications sustained in childbirth. Although she didn't live to forty and had to contend with immense hardship throughout her life, Wollstonecraft's influence on the development of literary and cultural history, both as a writer and as a mother, would echo across generations.

READING LIST:
Feminist Fiction

1. **FANTOMINA; OR, LOVE IN A MAZE** by Eliza Haywood (birthday unknown)

2. **THE AWAKENING** by Kate Chopin (Aquarius)

3. **THE WRONGS OF WOMAN; OR, MARIA** by Mary Wollstonecraft (Taurus)

4. **IOLA LEROY; OR, SHADOWS UPLIFTED** by Frances Ellen Watkins Harper (Libra)

5. **ZAMI: A NEW SPELLING OF MY NAME: A BIOMYTHOGRAPHY** by Audre Lorde (Aquarius)

CASE STUDY #2: J. M. BARRIE

Sir James Matthew Barrie, 1st Baronet, as he would be known later in his life, was born in the Scottish town of Kirriemuir on May 8, 1860. He was one of ten children, two of whom died in infancy. His father was a weaver. His mother, Margaret Ogilvy, had lost her own mother at the age of eight and had taken on her mother's household duties; Barrie would later include a memoir of his mother's youth in the 1896 book *Margaret Ogilvy* and would meditate on the theme of motherhood before its time through the character of Wendy in the universe of *Peter Pan*.

Sadly, Margaret's abbreviated childhood was not the only trauma that would haunt Barrie's contribution to the canon of children's literature. When Barrie was six, his older brother, David, died in an ice-skating accident the day before his fourteenth birthday. The family's grief following this loss, and the image of a golden boy never growing up, had a deep and lasting influence on Barrie's creative work.

As a child, Barrie wrote and produced plays with his friends in the washhouse across from his family's home. An early play, *Bandolero the Bandit*, was performed while Barrie was still a student. Barrie turned his attention to journalism while in college, moved to London, and wrote for the page and the stage. His success put him in touch with illustrious contemporaries including Thomas Hardy (Gemini), Robert Louis Stevenson (Scorpio), and H. G. Wells (Virgo). Barrie married an actress, Mary Ansell (Pisces), who was the lead in one of his plays, and gave her a St. Bernard dog. The marriage was childless, and possibly sexless, and would end in divorce.

Barrie was a prolific and celebrated writer all his life, but *Peter Pan*, the universe he developed in a series of novels and plays, would be his legacy. The works were inspired in part by the Llewellyn Davies boys, George (Cancer), Jack (Virgo), Peter (Pisces), Michael (Gemini), and Nicholas (Sagittarius). Barrie befriended the eldest of these brothers during his frequent visits to Kensington Gardens, then bonded with their mother,

Sylvia Llewellyn Davies (Sagittarius), after meeting her at a dinner party. Notably, Sylvia's niece was Daphne du Maurier (Taurus), who would grow up to become the writer famous for the Gothic romance novel *Rebecca*. The Barries and the Llewellyn Davieses went on to become close family friends, with "Uncle Jim" supporting Sylvia following the death of her husband, Arthur (Pisces), then becoming one of the boys' guardians following Sylvia's death.

What kind of grown man befriends children at the park and then goes on to become their guardian? While some have tried to read Barrie's friendships with children as sinister, accounts suggest there was probably nothing sexual or sexualizing in his attentions. (In fact, it seems likely that if J. M. Barrie were alive today, he might identify as asexual.) Rather, we might understand Barrie as an unusual person who, in both his art and his life, clung to childhood and wrestled with the notion of its ending.

This preoccupation was likely informed by Barrie's own traumatic experiences; when he wrote, in the novel *Peter and Wendy*, that "all children, except one, grow up," it is possible that he was thinking about his brother. Indeed, Barrie's novels and plays have a dark, sad, cutting edge that doesn't always appear in pop-culture adaptations of *Peter Pan*. It is also possible that, by befriending children, Barrie was seeking out alternate roles in which he could help to raise them, roles that did not involve the act of physical procreation. Notably, when Barrie died, he left the *Peter Pan* copyright to a children's hospital in London, ensuring that the art made from his deepest wound would continue to benefit children in need.

An image from a 1905 production of *Peter Pan*, the play.

New York Public Library
Digital Collections

While J. M. Barrie was most likely just a weirdo, not a creep, we may ask whether making someone else's children into public figures is ever really appropriate. It's unclear whether the Llewellyn Davies brothers appreciated being associated with Peter Pan throughout their lives; in fact, Peter Llewellyn Davies once referred to Barrie's work as "that terrible masterpiece." While the loyal intensity Taurus brings to relationships of all kinds can be a truly powerful force for good, it can also be a bit much, as when the little man with the big dog from the park is suddenly asking you to dress as pirates and act out an adventure for a photo album. While Taurus writers can become deeply inspired by the people they love and should lean into that inspiration, it's important not to get so swept up in this inspiration that you lose sight of the person who provoked it in the first place. Or perhaps that's precisely what J. M. Barrie was doing—refusing to lose sight of his brother, David, by finding him in the faces of the children around him and transforming him into an immortal child who never grows up. Read this way, Barrie presents a brilliant, if tragic, figure.

Whether Barrie's immortal work came from love or grief or both, we should note that there are other Tauruses who made lasting contributions to the literature of childhood, including L. Frank Baum of *Wizard of Oz* fame and Dodie Smith, who wrote *The Hundred and One Dalmatians*.

CASE STUDY #3: CHARLOTTE BRONTË

Taurus queen Charlotte Brontë was born on April 21, 1816, the third daughter of Maria and Patrick Brontë. Her father was a curate; when Charlotte was four, he moved the family to the Yorkshire village of Haworth to work at the local church. Surrounded by the windswept moors familiar from her sister Emily Brontë's *Wuthering Heights* (Leo, see page 118), Haworth's cobbled streets wind uphill; the parsonage, as well as the churchyard, sit above the other dwelling places. This meant that, while the water at the parsonage may have been relatively safe to

drink, the water in much of the village
was contaminated, and death haunted
Haworth like a specter. Add to that the
ghostly landscape and early deaths of
Charlotte Brontë's mother and two
older sisters, and it is no wonder her
fictional heroines skate the darkness
at the edges of their worlds.

**YOU MIGHT BE
A TAURUS IF:**
you love to edit
others' work.

Along with her younger sisters,
Emily (Leo) and Anne (Capricorn), and
their older brother, Branwell (Cancer),
Charlotte produced an intense body of juvenilia set within a shared narrative universe. At first, the young writers cohabitated in the imaginary world
of Glass Town, but Emily and Anne created a version of the world called
Gondal while Charlotte and Branwell developed Angria. In the juvenilia we
see the strength of the siblings' creative bonds as well as the boundlessness
of their imaginations. We also see a palimpsest of sorts: a fantasy world
overlying the grim reality of all that had been and would be lost.

Charlotte and Emily followed their older sisters to Cowan Bridge
School, then returned after their older sisters died. These deaths may have
been caused or hastened by poor conditions at the school, and the idea
that schools were not always safe, healthy places for young girls would
come up in Charlotte's fiction. Charlotte left home again to attend Roe
Head School, before working there as a teacher while Emily and Anne
attended as students. Charlotte also traveled to Brussels as a pupil and
then returned as a teacher. The sense that she was the teacher in the
group—a profoundly Taurean conviction—may have carried over to
Charlotte's editing and promotion of her younger sisters' works after
their deaths. For example, in developing Emily's brand, Charlotte dis-
entangled some of her early poetry from the narrative world of their
shared mythology in order to make it seem emotional, sentimental, and

self-expressive. Put another way, Charlotte would later turn Emily into one of her Victorian heroines.

In 1846, Charlotte, Emily, and Anne published a volume of poems under the masculine but somewhat androgynous pen names Currer, Ellis, and Acton Bell. The following year, their three great novels appeared: Charlotte's *Jane Eyre*, Anne's *Agnes Grey*, and Emily's *Wuthering Heights*. While even a quick summary of *Jane Eyre* would demonstrate the depth of Charlotte's engagement with women's precarity and the colonial injustices haunting even the most domestic sites of British life, we wouldn't want to spoil the book for you. If you haven't read it and have somehow managed to avoid spoilers, don't press your luck. Stop what you're doing, put this book down, and go read *Jane Eyre*. We'll be here when you get back.

The family's literary triumph of 1846 was, sadly, short-lived. Emily, Anne, and Branwell all died between 1848 and 1849, most likely of tuberculosis, though the sisters had, in a sense, lost Branwell to alcoholism well before this time. Charlotte was left holding the bag full of Emily's and Anne's artistic aspirations. With a bull's steadfastness, loyalty, and downright stubbornness, she set about defining the family's literary reputation, and went on to publish two more novels in her lifetime, *Shirley* (1849) and *Villette* (1853). While *Villette* bears many similarities to *Jane Eyre*, *Shirley* is a bit messier and more abrasive, and the landscape functions as a kind of character. Women's literature expert Lauren Burke has wondered whether *Shirley* might have been Emily Brontë's mysterious second novel; we know she was working on one when she died, but it is believed to be lost. It is possible that Charlotte viewed completing and publishing the book as an act of loyalty to her sister's desires, much the same way she might have adopted and raised a child left orphaned by Emily's death.

Charlotte married Arthur Bell Nicholls (Capricorn) in 1854, but their marriage lasted only nine months. The cause of Charlotte's early death was most likely complications sustained in pregnancy. A final novel, *The Professor*, appeared posthumously a few years later.

CODA: JESSIE REDMON FAUSET

Tauruses often occupy the position of the stubborn aesthetes of the zodiac. A Venus-ruled sign, Taurus has an eye for beauty and a taste for luxury, but these bulls are not typically known for their flexibility. When stubbornness and an insistence on aesthetics combine, you can end up with people who know exactly what they want and how to make it happen. This makes for very interesting artists, but it can also produce editors and tastemakers gifted with a bird's-eye view of an era and a keen sense of how to direct it. Such is the case with Jessie Redmon Fauset, who was not only one of the most prolific writers of the Harlem Renaissance, but also instrumental in the discovery and nurturing of some of its most important writers.

The daughter of an African Methodist Episcopal minister, Fauset had a difficult childhood marked by poverty and the early loss of both parents. She graduated at the top of her high-school class and went on to earn a BA in classical languages from Cornell University. Originally, Fauset had wanted to attend Bryn Mawr College; at the time, it was typical for the valedictorian of her high school be awarded an acceptance to the college, but Fauset was refused a place based on her race. Instead, Fauset would graduate from not one, but two Ivy League universities, and would earn a certificate from the Sorbonne in Paris as well. When a Taurus decides to accomplish something, there is very little that can stand in their way. Oh, and did we mention that Fauset was also one of the first African American women to graduate Phi Beta Kappa and the first woman ever to do so from Cornell?

After Cornell, Fauset worked as a high school French and Latin teacher (classical languages are Venusian subjects) until she was recruited by W. E. B. Du Bois (Pisces, see page 260) to serve as the literary editor at *The Crisis*, the official literary magazine of the NAACP. While at *The Crisis*, Fauset championed countless Black authors who would go on to become some of the greatest voices of modernist fiction and poetry, including Anne Spencer (Aquarius, see page 242), Langston Hughes (Aquarius), Countee Cullen (Gemini), and Jean Toomer (Capricorn, see page 215). Tauruses like to excel, and their bullish stamina means that they often do exactly that. However, they almost always insist on doing so quietly and with a degree of modesty. That Venus rulership means there is a delicacy about them just beneath all that bluster.

While editing *The Crisis*, Fauset also worked closely with Du Bois on *The Brownies' Book*. However, Fauset wasn't just an editor. She wrote her own fiction, criticism, and essays in which she dealt with issues of race, class, and feminism. She also published four novels, *There Is Confusion* (1924), *Plum Bun* (1928), *The Chinaberry Tree: A Novel of American Life* (1931), and *Comedy, American Style* (1933), before ceasing to write completely.

In 1926, Fauset left *The Crisis* and went back to teaching for good. Sometimes a Taurus needs to step out of the limelight. Despite their formidable presence, bulls can be shy, and too much focus can sometimes cause them to retreat. In 1929, Fauset married Herbert Harris, an insurance broker, to whom she stayed married until his death. Fauset died in Philadelphia in 1961 at the age of seventy-nine. Although she may not be remembered as readily as some of her contemporaries, she was a trailblazing writer and a brilliant editor who was instrumental in the Harlem Renaissance becoming the groundbreaking artistic movement that it was.

NOTES FOR WRITERS WITH OTHER TAURUS PLACEMENTS

WRITER'S CORNER

POSITIVE ASPECTS

Taurus writers can draw inspiration from their personal connections, can stick with projects for as long as is necessary, and finish what they start.

NEGATIVE ASPECTS

Self-indulgence.

WRITER BEWARE

Honor your obsessions, sure, but make sure you don't get stuck in a whirlpool that isn't helping you or your art.

TAURUS MOON: You are fiercely independent yet simultaneously incredibly supportive of others. You don't like being told what to do and that can mean thinking carefully about criticism: when to take it and when to dismiss it. You tend to be the person others turn to when they are in trouble, and you might think about serving as a mentor to other writers.

TAURUS RISING: You may struggle with the seemingly divergent impulses to create beautiful art and make sure you are financially stable. You have a gift for language and may tend toward writing that is elegant at the sentence level. Your fierce determination to succeed can sometimes be at odds with your desire to make art for art's sake.

MERCURY IN TAURUS: As a writer, you have an excellent memory and are the consummate observer. You may get ideas from people-watching, and you are remarkably adept at ferreting out the deeper motives behind people's actions—a skill that can serve you tremendously in your writing. You may have a tendency to turn a blind eye toward word repetition in your writing, so be mindful.

VENUS IN TAURUS: You are all about the process of writing. An aesthete down to the bone, you have a love of every kind of art, something that can help raise your writing to the next level. You are careful and exacting with your language, and because you are so inspired by beauty, it might serve you to have a touch of luxury to adorn your workspace.

MARS IN TAURUS: You're a hard worker and can be a touch opinionated, but because you have a quiet and constant work ethic and an ability to tackle large projects, that opinionated streak can be used to your advantage to maintain consistency of purpose and tone over the duration of a longer work.

TRY THIS!

+ WRITE a poem from the perspective of someone you love.

+ OUTLINE a story but base the plot entirely on relationship dynamics.

+ WRITE a work of flash fiction set in an imaginative world you remember from childhood.

READER'S CORNER:
COMPATIBILITY CHART

Which Taurus-composed book is most likely to appeal to you? It depends on your sign. Look for your match below. And don't forget to look at your rising and Moon signs if you know those.

SIGN	CLASSIC	MODERN
ARIES	MIKHAIL BULGAKOV, *Heart of a Dog*	JOY HARJO, *Poet Warrior: A Memoir*
TAURUS	DAPHNE DU MAURIER, *Rebecca*	LING MA, *Severance*
GEMINI	VLADIMIR NABOKOV, *Transparent Things*	ANDREY KURKOV, *Death and the Penguin*
CANCER	HARPER LEE, *To Kill a Mockingbird*	MARTHA NUSSBAUM, *Upheavals of Thought: The Intelligence of Emotions*
LEO	DANTE GABRIEL ROSSETTI, *Ballads and Sonnets*	CATHERYNNE M. VALENTE, *Comfort Me with Apples*
VIRGO	NOVALIS, *Hymns to the Night*	NAOMI KLEIN, *The Shock Doctrine: The Rise of Disaster Capitalism*

SIGN	CLASSIC	MODERN
LIBRA	CHARLOTTE BRONTË, *Shirley*	NORA EPHRON, *I Feel Bad About My Neck and Other Thoughts on Being a Woman*
SCORPIO	LORRAINE HANSBERRY, *A Raisin in the Sun*	LOUISE GLÜCK, *Winter Recipes from the Collective*
SAGITTARIUS	WILLIAM SHAKESPEARE, *Twelfth Night*	SAMANTHA HUNT, *The Unwritten Book: An Investigation*
CAPRICORN	ANTHONY TROLLOPE, *The Claverings*	CORETTA SCOTT KING, *Coretta: My Life, My Love, My Legacy*
AQUARIUS	HENRY FIELDING, *Shamela*	ANGELA CARTER, *The Bloody Chamber*
PISCES	HONORÉ DE BALZAC, *Séraphîta*	YUSEF KOMUNYAKAA, *Thieves of Paradise*

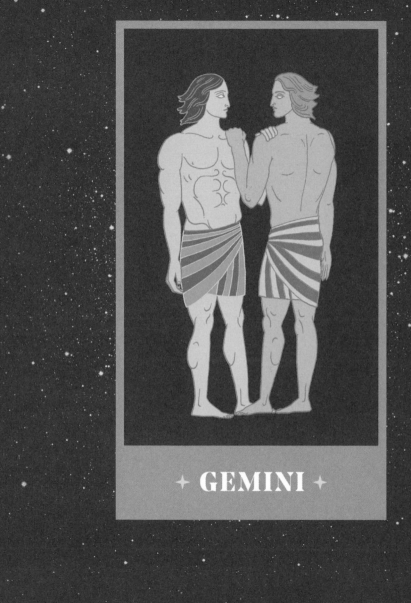

GEMINI

GEMINI

THE QUIXOTIC WRITER

I CONTAIN MULTITUDES.

—Walt Whitman

GEMINI 101

Gemini's symbol is the twins, and it's often said that inside every solitary Gemini there exists two completely different people, each with their own likes, agendas, and intentions. The constellation Gemini is composed of the stars Castor and Pollux, twins from Greek and Roman mythology. In one iteration of their legend, Pollux was so grief-stricken upon his brother's death that Zeus granted the twins the ability to share their time on Earth, one residing in the heavens and one living among men, switching off at regular intervals. The moment of that switch—that beat when one twin leaves and the other slips in, complete with their own value system and goals—*that* is what it means to be a Gemini. If that sounds confusing for those who deal with a Gemini, imagine trying to be one.

Geminis tend to do things in pairs. They often oscillate between two different career paths, and in romance, they are not typically known for monogamy (though this may be most true for those with Venus in Gemini); they are more than one person, so perhaps they should have more than one lover as well. Because Gemini rules the 3rd House, the home of siblings, even their love affairs can take on a sibling dynamic. Geminis are always in search of their missing twins and have been known to seek out that sibling connection in strange places—with bosses, romantic partners, romantic partners' spouses . . . Gemini's system of morality often sits decidedly outside the realm of conventional ethics.

SIGN OVERVIEW

SYMBOL:
The Twins

ELEMENT: Air

QUALITY: Mutable

HOUSE RULED:
3rd (Communication,
Siblings, Immediate
Environment)

PLANETARY RULER:
Mercury

POSITIVE TRAITS:
Fun, Charming,
Adaptable

NEGATIVE TRAITS:
Distractible, Glib,
Superficial

The sign of Gemini has earned a reputation for being fickle, disingenuous, or indulgently mercurial, but this is often a mischaracterization. Some of this misapprehension of the sign stems from the fact that it is ruled by the planet Mercury. Mercury is about speed, travel, mental processing, and communication. It imbues Gemini with a gift for language and an ability to do everything with an enviable quickness. This also makes them changeable—and not just changeable, but suddenly changeable. Geminis can firmly believe one thing and then firmly believe its opposite a short while later. This can be misunderstood as, well, lying, but Geminis don't mean to lie. They genuinely believe what they say while they're saying it. They just don't feel the need to pretend not to change their minds about those things. And change their minds they will! This can sometimes be a deal breaker for people who demand consistency or strict adherence to rules (we're looking at you, Virgos). But if you're the type to value rules above all else, then you should probably avoid these tricksters from the get-go.

THE GEMINI WRITER:

A LITERARY HISTORY

Geminis tend to occupy liminal spaces, flitting between two worlds, and are often in possession of two totally different identities. Arthur Conan Doyle was a medical doctor, but he was also a writer and a lecturer. Walt Whitman was a poet, but he was also a volunteer nurse. Amelia Edwards was a polymath with a passion for Egyptology, and Thomas Hardy was a gifted architect before devoting himself to fiction . . . which he then dropped for poetry. All four were interested in both art and science, with a heaping side of mysticism.

CASE STUDY #1: ARTHUR CONAN DOYLE

How can someone who believes in medicine and the scientific method also believe in fairies? And how can a writer who created the ultimate model of rational thought in Sherlock Holmes also believe wholeheartedly in séances and spiritualism? How can one person hold these seemingly opposite and conflicting ideas? How does he reconcile the dissonance? The answer, of course, is that he doesn't have to. Because he's a Gemini.

Arthur Conan Doyle (born May 22, 1859) was born in England to Irish parents, the third oldest of nine children. His early life was troubled and unstable, with young Conan Doyle often living in poverty under the tyranny of an alcoholic father. Rising above his meager beginnings, he went on to attend Stonyhurst College and studied medicine at University of Edinburgh Medical School where he was trained by

YOU
MIGHT BE
A GEMINI IF:
you see two sides
to every story . . .
and then two sides to
each of those sides . . .
and then . . .

Fairy Offering Posy of Harebells to Elsie, the fourth Cottingley Fairies photograph. Photograph by Elsie Wright and Frances Griffiths.

the famous Scottish surgeon Dr. Joseph Bell (Sagittarius). Bell would later serve as the model for Conan Doyle's most famous character, Sherlock Holmes. In true Gemini fashion, however, Arthur Conan Doyle was never content to settle into a single profession.

Conan Doyle began writing early in his life but wouldn't find any real success with the profession until he broke through with the 1887 publication of *A Study in Scarlet,* in which he introduced the world to the unforgettable Sherlock Holmes. Conan Doyle eventually stopped practicing medicine and concentrated on writing, but not before taking a detour into spiritualism. Geminis love a good detour, and this one would prove so significant that he became one of the spiritualism movement's greatest and most vocal proponents. He wrote books and gave lectures on the subject. When Agatha Christie (Virgo) briefly disappeared in 1926, unlike his fellow mystery writer Dorothy L. Sayers (Gemini), who set out to solve the mystery of Christie's disappearance by following clues and conducting a crime scene investigation, Conan Doyle sought the help of a psychic to assist with the search. Conan Doyle also famously took on the cause of the Cottingley Fairy photos. The photos, fairly obvious fakes, were the work of two young cousins, Elsie Wright and Frances Griffiths. Although the girls would later admit their fairies were merely cutouts posed among flowers, Conan Doyle fell for the ruse hook, line, and sinker. Geminis are born with their capacity for suspension of disbelief ramped up to eleven.

Gemini is the sign of alter egos, of doubles, of doppelgängers. The very fact that Arthur Conan Doyle has become almost synonymous with Sherlock Holmes is the essence of Gemini. This twinning is a Gemini trait, and through this alter ego, Holmes, Conan Doyle expresses many Gemini characteristics, themes, and interests. Holmes is eccentric, quicknatured, and flamboyant, and his preoccupations are varied, speaking to the Gemini habit of picking up a little bit of everything. Geminis are the buffet-purveyors of knowledge. They would like a little bit from forensics, a little bit from music theory, just a dollop of art history, and why not also add in some boxing? Of course, Holmes's depth of knowledge far surpasses any Gemini's, but in order to create such a character, the author himself must dip a toe into all these disciplines. And then there is Holmes's penchant for disguises! Geminis love dressing up and pretending to be people they are not. They also don't turn their noses up at the prospect of bending the truth just a tad, as Holmes is wont to do whenever it is in the interest of a case.

Most scholars locate the inception of detective fiction with the creation of Le Chevalier C. Auguste Dupin, Edgar Allan Poe's (Capricorn, see page 219) fictional creation, but Sherlock Holmes has certainly exceeded Dupin in terms of fame and influence. Leave it to a Capricorn to invent the concept of ratiocination (the process of deductive reasoning that leads to a precise and exact conclusion, and a defining aspect of Holmes's character), but leave it to a Gemini to blab to everyone about it. The only thing Geminis love more than puzzling over something is talking about how they've been puzzling over something. Any audience will do, and in Dr. John Watson, his famous sidekick, Holmes has an ideal chatting partner. If only all Geminis were furnished with such an interlocutor at birth, they would never need to turn to vice. (Except in Holmes's case, in which he also turned to vice. As we shall see, Geminis contain multitudes.)

READING LIST:

Early Mysteries

1. THINGS AS THEY ARE; OR, THE ADVENTURES OF CALEB WILLIAMS by William Godwin (Aries)

2. "THE MURDERS IN THE RUE MORGUE" by Edgar Allan Poe (Capricorn)

3. "THE DEAD LETTER" by Metta Victoria Fuller Victor (Pisces), writing as Seeley Regester

4. A STUDY IN SCARLET by Arthur Conan Doyle (Gemini)

Despite the extreme popularity of Sherlock Holmes, in 1893 Conan Doyle published "The Final Problem," which saw the iconic detective murdered by his nemesis, Moriarty. Conan Doyle simply went full Gemini and killed off his alter ego. Can you blame him? After all, there were ghosts to summon and fairies to chase. When "The Final Problem" was published, public outcry was extreme. People even wore black armbands in mourning. In 1901, however, Conan Doyle brought back his iconic detective in the novel *The Hound of the Baskervilles*. This is perhaps the most classic example of the Gemini nature of Conan Doyle's work. This sign is impulsive, yet if they go too far, they are, thankfully, changeable. Can you imagine a Capricorn changing their mind about something as extreme as this? No, you can't. Because Capricorns are too busy making lists and considering world domination. And what does a Gemini think about their reputation after acting so impulsively, so quixotically? They absolutely do not care. Not one iota. Because Geminis believe that changing their mind half a billion times is their birthright.

By the end of Conan Doyle's life, he had written sixty short stories, twenty-two novels, and thirteen books on spiritualism, created one of the most iconic and influential characters of all time, traveled the world, had a successful practice as a medical doctor, and was still so wound up after a tour to promote his most recent spiritualism book—a tour his doctor had advised against—that he died quite suddenly of a heart attack. Geminis always know how to make an exit.

CASE STUDY #2: AMELIA EDWARDS

If Gemini men are the flamboyant disrupters of the zodiac, Gemini women are the pixie explorers. Although less well known than her male Gemini counterparts, Amelia Edwards was a pioneering adventurer who took the classic Gemini need for freedom to the extreme. Born in 1831 in London, Edwards received no formal education but flourished in the arts under her mother's direction. Edwards published poetry by age seven and a short story when she was only twelve. She was remarkably gifted at the visual arts as well, even catching the attention of Charles Dickens's (Aquarius, see page 245) illustrator George Cruikshank (also Aquarius). When her interest in painting was discouraged by her parents, Edwards began composing music, but her passion waned after an illness damaged her vocal cords. Geminis often excel in the arts, flitting from one medium to another, but they are propelled by a sense of fun and adventure. The second that fun disappears from the scene, so does the Gemini.

While a Gemini might leave when things are
no longer fun, don't worry. They'll bring the fun
with them wherever they go.

At the age of twenty, Edwards published her first novel, *My Brother's Wife* (1855), to great success, but it was her scandalous tale of bigamy, *Barbara's History* (1864), that provided her first major success. Geminis are often tricksters, and nothing thrills them as much as delivering a good shock every once in a while, just to shake things up. Edwards's ability to tell a sensationalist tale and tell it well would prove incredibly profitable. She published eight novels in all before changing direction once again. While some authors let their careers peter out, Edwards chose to stop writing novels at the top of her game. Her final novel, *Lord Brackenbury* (1880), was an enormous commercial success, but after publishing it, she dropped fiction altogether and abruptly shifted her attention to travel writing.

When Edwards's parents died shortly before she turned thirty, she used her considerable earnings to set out and see the world. A queer writer, Edwards took her partner, Ellen Braysher (Aries), along with her on her travels, and together the two women embarked on a series of exploratory adventures, which Edwards then wrote about and published. They continued this way for many years until, during a trip down the Nile River, Edwards became enamored with Egyptology. After writing her final travel book, she devoted herself to conservation efforts, intent on promoting the scientific investigation of the Egyptian ruins and promoting Egyptian archeology in general. She lectured, wrote books on the subject, and raised funds for the cause. With a friend, Reginald Stuart Poole (Aquarius), she started the Egypt Exploration Fund.

Amelia Edwards's writing is marked by the vibrant curiosity and hunger for knowledge that is typical of the Gemini writer. Her travel writing evinces an openness and ebullience of spirit, if still mired in the colonialist gaze typical of the genre at the time. She greets people from other cultures as equals, but there is still the sense of the collector about her (Geminis can be single-minded about an obsession for as long as it strikes their fancy). Still, this attitude is no doubt preferable to colonialist-minded travel writers of the same era—think Henry Morton Stanley (Aquarius) and his deeply problematic and Eurocentric depictions of the people of the Congo Basin.

Edwards was eclectic in her writing, moving deftly between fiction, narrative nonfiction, and essays. Her writing on Egypt shows a genuine love for the topic, and her knowledge of archeology is impressive. Geminis are known for acquiring vast amounts of knowledge rather quickly. Whether they can maintain it over the long haul is another matter entirely. But it is in her fiction that we see some of Edwards's most Gemini tendencies.

Undoubtedly, her most widely read piece of fiction is "The Phantom Coach" (1882), a tale often anthologized in ghost-story collections. "The Phantom Coach" is a tale about a man who gets lost in a snowstorm and takes shelter at the residence of a mysterious hermit who seemingly possesses occult knowledge. It is deeply Gemini on many levels.

First, Edwards's hero in the "The Phantom Coach" is for some reason twenty miles away from his home and completely unprepared for a snowstorm (Geminis tend to dislike preparation). Second, when the narrator arrives at the stranger's house, he simply invites himself to stay for the night, shocking the owner with his overfamiliarity. Aside from perhaps Sagittarius or Aquarius, Gemini is the sign most likely to inform you that it's cool—they're just going to crash on your sofa for a few days. It's snowing outside! Don't be so uptight! Third, while at the house, the main character becomes fascinated by a mysterious chamber filled with haunting curios. The room and its contents are a Gemini's dream. Edwards describes it as being filled with "geological specimens, surgical preparations, crucibles, retorts, and jars of chemicals . . . a model of a solar system, a small galvanic battery, and a microscope . . . maps, casts, papers, tracings, and learned lumber of all conceivable kinds." If one were to excavate a Gemini's mind, we hazard it might look strikingly similar to that fascinating yet cluttered room.

Finally, after chatting with the hermit and looking through all his artifacts, the narrator suddenly changes his mind (Gemini!) and decides to try to make it home. It has stopped snowing, you see, and the narrator has already satisfied his curiosity about the hermit and his baubles, and now it seems he must leave immediately (Geminis are arguably the most impatient sign). We won't tell you what happens when he sets out. We're not going to blab it all like a couple of blabby Geminis. We won't spoil the ending of the story for you, but you can be sure that, in classic Gemini fashion, it's tricksy.

After a varied career filled with twists and turns, and a characteristically Geminian penchant for flouting convention, Amelia Edwards succumbed to the flu in 1892, only three months after the death of her partner. Although mostly lost to history, Amelia Edwards's writing is worth another look. Geminis tend to pop back up when you least expect them.

CASE STUDY #3: WALT WHITMAN

Whitman was born on Long Island, New York, to struggling parents. His early life was marked by financial insecurity and chaos, presided over by an alcoholic father. He was forced to start working at the age of eleven. By seventeen, he was a teacher, but soon tired of the difficulty of the profession, especially under less-than-ideal circumstances. Whitman came into his own in his twenties when he found work as a journalist, eventually starting a newspaper. Known for his volatile, contradictory views, often taking radical positions on issues like women's property rights, immigration, and labor, Whitman was something of a nineteenth-century bad boy. Geminis love courting controversy and delight in provoking others with their iconoclastic bombast. The knowledge that they can go back on any one of their unpopular opinions at the slightest inclination allows them to say and do things a more conservative sign might avoid.

As a poet, Whitman didn't have immediate success, publishing his seminal work, *Leaves of Grass,* to minimal attention in 1855. A controversial work that broke with tradition (both poetic and moralistic), *Leaves of Grass* trafficked in sensuality and Transcendentalism. Inspired by an essay titled "The Poet," written by the Transcendentalist writer Ralph

Waldo Emerson (also a Gemini), *Leaves of Grass* was a groundbreaking, innovative work that didn't conform to the established poetic standards of the day. Emerson, though, was a fan and helped popularize the work. He praised it, declaring it "the most extraordinary piece of wit and wisdom that America has yet contributed" and writing that it contained "incomparable things said incomparably well." It's no surprise that it was another Gemini who helped Whitman reach his intended audience. Geminis tend to travel in packs and support one another. The reason for this is unknown. Is it uncomplicated altruism? Perhaps a desire to focus the blame on someone else who is also trying to cause a scene? Or is it purely based on interest in similar themes?

Whitman also had a stint in a second career of sorts, working as a volunteer nurse during the Civil War and treating between eighty thousand and one hundred thousand patients. He never married, and while his personal life remains something of a mystery, over the years his reputation has flourished into that of a bona fide queer icon. His sensualist poems often sing the praises of young, beautiful men, and he had a deeply romantic (though possibly unrequited) relationship with a Confederate soldier named Peter Doyle (Gemini). He never openly declared himself gay—something that would have been taboo at the time.

Throughout his life, Whitman broke with convention in a typically Gemini fashion. Shocking others, prioritizing freedom, living as a queer writer and an iconoclast, he would go on to inspire similarly inclined writers for generations to come.

When one considers the arduous, focus-oriented, often daunting task of revision, Gemini writers aren't usually the first people to spring to mind. We think Balzac (Taurus), Proust (Cancer), or even Flaubert (Sagittarius), with their obsessive need for perfectionism and insistence on *le mot juste*. Geminis tend to be more slapdash, and it's usually difficult to make them sit down and perfect anything. Besides, what's the point in perfecting something when you're just going to change your mind about it later anyway? As Whitman himself writes, "Do I contradict myself? / Very well then I contradict myself, / (I am large, I contain multitudes.)" But it is precisely this mutability that makes Whitman's writing so incredibly Gemini in nature.

Initially, *Leaves of Grass* contained only twelve poems. When he had more poems in his arsenal, another writer might simply have published a second book, but not Whitman. Instead, he just kept revising and adding to that initial book until it contained 383 poems and had been released in nine editions. Although attention to detail isn't usually a skill in most Geminis' wheelhouses, they do love to revise, especially when it's on their own terms. Partly this is because they've changed their minds since originally drafting a piece, and partly it is because they find it fun to play with stuff they've already made—like turning their Lego castle into a battleship. But while most Geminis are guilty of this, Walt Whitman stands head and shoulders above the rest.

Do you like digressions? We hope so! Because there is no one chattier than a Gemini. And when they're chatting, they are less apt to follow a train of thought than they are to chase anything shiny that interests them. Whitman himself is often characterized as a *flaneur* (a glamorously lazy wanderer), but it is his lines of poetic verse that are the ultimate *flaneurs*. They will go where they want to, and convention be damned!

His meandering, digressive style was far from typical of the time. In general, the poetic devices that Whitman uses are often Gemini in nature. In his use of catalogues, he raises the list to new artistic heights (Geminis love to list and categorize things), and his anaphora (repeating the first word of a line) is hypnotically Gemini. Geminis are the child in the back seat asking, "Are we there yet?" repeatedly until you let them out of the car so they can run around. Similarly, Whitman's content is Geminian. *Leaves of Grass* expresses an openness to the new, a desire to communicate with any and all, and a multitude of themes, jumping about from America, to equality, to love, to the self, to the lack of boundaries between the self and others, to a taboo elevation of the human body, to sexuality, to Abraham Lincoln, to a metatextual nod to the book itself.

> Where are we going, Walt Whitman?
> The doors close in an hour.
> Which way does your beard point tonight?
>
> —ALLEN GINSBERG (GEMINI)

Because *Leaves of Grass* defied convention, it also defied description, confusing critics and antagonizing the establishment, which perceived its self-agency and experimentation as not just disgraceful, but a threat to the status quo. Critics tended to react to *Leaves of Grass* as if it needed to be put in the corner for a time-out. (*What are you doing telling everyone that they have bodies? You're not supposed to talk about that!*) The work was instantly polarizing. While some, like Emerson, reacted to Whitman's work with excitement, others condemned it completely. Sometimes the reactions verged on personal attacks, with Ezra Pound (Scorpio) ultimately declaring of Whitman, "He is disgusting. He is an exceedingly nauseating pill."

During the twentieth century, Whitman's reputation soared, and his writing that was previously seen as scandalous became enormously influential, especially on poets like Allen Ginsberg (Gemini), Langston Hughes (Aquarius), and Joy Harjo (Taurus). Many of the aspects of his writing that we came to appreciate and integrate into modern poetry are the most Gemini aspects of *Leaves of Grass*. In "When I Read a Book," Whitman speaks of not knowing the self, an endless source of interest to the Gemini. This self-excavation continues in his most famous poem, "Song of Myself," which includes lines like: "I celebrate myself, and sing myself," and "Walt Whitman, a kosmos, of Manhattan the son / Turbulent, fleshy, sensual, eating, drinking, and breeding." In "Shut Not Your Doors," Whitman calls attention to the book itself. He writes, "a book I have made, The words of my book nothing, the drift of it every thing." This kind of reflexive, almost metafictional view presaged postmodernism, but it's also very Gemini to point out what's happening in the moment, even if it's awkward. When there is an uncomfortable silence at Thanksgiving dinner, a Gemini is the first to call attention to it and turn it into an (admittedly) even more uncomfortable joke.

Whitman died of pneumonia in 1892. He was an inscrutable character and an innovative, incendiary, gloriously original writer who changed the trajectory of poetry forever, but one doesn't get the sense that he really meant to, nor that he necessarily cared. Or maybe he did. Who knows? He did, after all, contain multitudes.

CODA: THOMAS HARDY

Geminis like to combine their talents, and Thomas Hardy was no exception. Perhaps most famous these days for his classic novel *Far from the Madding Crowd* (1874), Hardy seamlessly interweaves several of his interests, skills, and passions into his work, from architecture to science to social justice. Possessed by an ardent love of music and a gift for harmony, Hardy's musical lyricism is evident not only in his prose style, but often in his narrative choices and even structure. Indeed, specific pieces of music within Hardy's work often serve as foreshadowing.

Like many Geminis, Hardy wasn't content to have just one career. During his lifetime he was a poet, an Anglican priest, a novelist, and even a successful architect. After an illness, Hardy died of a heart attack on January 11, 1928. A disagreement about where Hardy ought to be buried led to his ashes being interred in Westminster Abbey, while his heart was buried in Stinsford with his wife. You'd be hard-pressed to find something more Gemini than having your heart and your body buried in completely different locations.

NOTES FOR WRITERS WITH OTHER GEMINI PLACEMENTS

WRITER'S CORNER

POSITIVE ASPECTS

You are great at revisions. The chance to do something twice is a Gemini's dream.

NEGATIVE ASPECTS

You can get distracted easily. Try to limit your access to shiny new things while working on a beloved project.

WRITER BEWARE

Check your facts! Your mind moves a mile a minute. It's so fast, in fact, that you may miss a thing or two.

GEMINI MOON: You are emotionally resilient, which is perhaps the best quality for a writer to have when it comes to the business side of publishing. Every writer piles up rejection slips, but how quickly those rejections slide off a writer's back is often the key to how likely they are to find success. Your Moon in Gemini all but assures your longevity as a writer.

GEMINI RISING: You wear your cleverness on your sleeve and have a gift for saying (and writing) exactly what you mean. You might consider writing creative nonfiction. Others will appreciate the honesty with which you tackle your subjects.

MERCURY IN GEMINI: You are the epitome of clever. You know a little bit about everything and are a veritable repository of interesting facts. If you have any difficulty maintaining focus on longer projects, you may want to try writing in short bursts, because this Mercury placement gives you an almost miraculous ability to sprint. String enough writing sprints together and you walk away with a novel.

VENUS IN GEMINI: You have a light touch and a variety of interests. Blessed with an obvious gift for humor, you infuse your writing with wit, no matter the subject. Writers with Venus in Gemini delight in collecting interesting trivia and using it to great effect in their writing.

MARS IN GEMINI: Mars in Gemini writers crave adventure but with a heady dose of the philosophical. A marvelous duality informs your passions and can lead you to take on issues that another sign may avoid. Gemini's famous commitment issues can sometimes rear their ugly head with this placement, though, so make sure to work on follow-through. Your projects deserve your undivided attention.

TRY THIS!

+ MAKE a list of your top ten favorite words. Use each to inspire a poem or story.

+ WRITE a novel about a set of twins.

+ RESEARCH a scientific process you know little about. Use what you learn as a jumping-off point for a new project.

READER'S CORNER:
COMPATIBILITY CHART

Which Gemini-composed book is most likely to appeal to you? It depends on your sign. Look for your match below. And don't forget to look at your rising and Moon signs if you know those.

SIGN	CLASSIC	MODERN
ARIES	W. B. YEATS, *The Collected Poems of W. B. Yeats*	GWENDOLYN BROOKS, *Maud Martha*
TAURUS	THOMAS HARDY, *Far from the Madding Crowd*	SALMAN RUSHDIE, *Midnight's Children*
GEMINI	ARTHUR CONAN DOYLE, *The Hound of the Baskervilles*	KHADIJAH QUEEN, *I'm So Fine: A List of Famous Men and What I Had On*
CANCER	THOMAS HARDY, *Jude the Obscure*	LOUISE ERDRICH, *Love Medicine*
LEO	ARTHUR CONAN DOYLE, *A Study in Scarlet*	JOE HILL, *NOS4A2*
VIRGO	RALPH WALDO EMERSON, *Poems*	JAMAICA KINCAID, *Lucy*

SIGN	CLASSIC	MODERN
LIBRA	WALT WHITMAN, *Leaves of Grass*	RICK RIORDAN, *Percy Jackson and the Olympians*
SCORPIO	MARQUIS DE SADE, *Justine*	ALLEN GINSBERG, *Howl*
SAGITTARIUS	AMELIA EDWARDS, *Barbara's History*	FEDERICO GARCÍA LORCA, *Poet in New York*
CAPRICORN	RALPH WALDO EMERSON, *Society and Solitude*	ANNE FRANK, *The Diary of a Young Girl*
AQUARIUS	G. K. CHESTERTON, *The Man Who Was Thursday*	RACHEL CARSON, *Silent Spring*
PISCES	FERNANDO PESSOA, *The Book of Disquiet*	THIRII MYO KYAW MYINT, *The End of Peril, The End of Enmity, The End of Strife, A Haven*

+ CANCER +

CANCER

I HAD THREE CHAIRS IN MY HOUSE;
ONE FOR SOLITUDE, TWO FOR FRIENDSHIP,
THREE FOR SOCIETY.

—Henry David Thoreau

CANCER 101

As the sign ruled by the Moon and symbolized by the crab, Cancer is all about protection and that which is hidden. Because of its close relationship with lunar cycles, Cancer is associated with fertility and growth, mother-hood, and creation. Ruling the 4th House of home and family, Cancer has a reputation as something of a recluse, but that isn't necessarily the case. Cancers don't need to be within a physical home to feel at ease (although they do enjoy a good nap on the couch), but rather they bring the concept of home with them wherever they go. This is why they have such a gift for putting others at ease.

Cancers always seem to be drawn to a central figure (often a mother) around whom they orbit like the Moon orbits the Earth. That central person—whether a family member, a friend, or a teacher—is often rep-resentative of a creator figure. Cancers are always cognizant of their roots and their memories of gestation, whether literal or metaphorical. Although Cancers are often linked with food—and a good many Cancers know their way around a kitchen—food is often a literal expression of a drive to nurture. Cancers have an impulse to protect and feed those they love. Whether with macaroni and cheese or with kind words and philo-sophical ideas, they simply can't help but bestow their innermost riches on those they care about.

SIGN OVERVIEW

SYMBOL:
The Crab

ELEMENT: Water

QUALITY: Cardinal

HOUSE RULED:
4th (Home, Family)

PLANETARY RULER:
The Moon

POSITIVE TRAITS:
Affectionate, Protective,
Loyal

NEGATIVE TRAITS:
Possessive, Moody,
Overly Sensitive

In astrology, the Moon is the province of memory, and Cancer, as the sign of memory, is always being drawn back to the past, to former triumphs and buried sins—their own and others'. Cancers have notoriously good memories. This works out quite nicely for them in school, should they choose to take it seriously, as they can memorize great swaths of material that would make a less gifted classmate shudder. However, it can also prove to be one of their greatest weaknesses. Every failure, every slight, every cruel glance lingers in their mind, and they are unable to fully let it go. Kind of heart, Cancers forgive easily, but they never forget. And it isn't just the unpleasant things they remember—it's the wonderful times, the heights of emotion, those long afternoons with their lover, the joy of their child's first steps. Those memories persist so strongly in the Cancer mind that as the events themselves slip further away through time, even those happy memories can be imbued with a tinge of sadness. Cancer is the reason the word *wistful* was invented.

THE CANCER WRITER:
A LITERARY HISTORY

Cancer writers tend to live quietly but write loudly, often living unassuming, even gentle lives, but writing about death, sin, and civil disobedience. Henry David Thoreau set off on a radical hermitage while still remaining closely attached to his beloved family. Ann Radcliffe and Matthew "Monk" Lewis, two titans of the Gothic genre who also shared a birthday, represented diametrically opposed views on the difference between horror and terror, and yet they lived relatively unassuming lives. And finally, in Nathaniel Hawthorne we encounter a Cancer so haunted by the sins of his ancestors that he dedicated himself to seeking the divine.

CASE STUDY #1: HENRY DAVID THOREAU

Henry David Thoreau was born the third of four children in a close-knit family in Concord, Massachusetts. His family struggled financially until his uncle discovered a deposit of graphite and the Thoreaus opened a pencil factory. As a child, Thoreau was adventurous but also something of a loner. He delighted in long walks in the woods and evinced an early love of nature, most likely instilled in him by his mother. In addition to being stricken with persistent ill health during childhood, he was somewhat accident-prone, suffering a series of falls, being thrown from a cow, and even accidentally chopping off part of his toe with an axe. That ill health would follow him into early adulthood and beyond when tuberculosis forced him to take time off from college.

Thoreau attended Concord Academy, followed by Harvard College, where he proved gifted at languages. After college, he taught briefly but eventually left the profession because he couldn't stomach its insistence on corporal punishment. A Cancer, when gifted with a sentimental nature, abhors the infliction of physical violence perhaps more than any other sign, and across the board, Cancers have a soft spot for children. It's no wonder, then, that this form of discipline was the thing that drove him from teaching.

YOU MIGHT BE A CANCER IF:
you seem chill, but still waters run deep.

Perhaps surprisingly, Thoreau was skilled with his hands and a whiz at building things. For a time, Thoreau settled into working in his father's pencil factory, where he was responsible for instituting design changes that resulted in a superior product as well as for several other inventions that helped to improve the family business. These technical skills would follow him into adulthood, and even while living at Walden Pond, Thoreau still worked around town as a handyman, laying foundations and mending fences.

If you're a Cancer, it can help to ask yourself:
What am I building and who am I trying to protect?

In 1838, Thoreau and his brother, John, opened a school with the intention of thoroughly upending the current system of pedagogy. The school was coeducational (it counted Louisa May Alcott [Sagittarius] among its pupils), did not use the corporal punishment that he so vociferously opposed, and concentrated a great deal on the natural world. During that time, the two brothers took what would turn out to be a momentous trip up the Concord and Merrimack Rivers, camping out and sleeping under the stars. The experience would have a profound impact on Thoreau, and he would eventually be moved to write about it. Two years later, the brothers would have to close the school when John acquired tetanus while shaving and became ill.

Although Cancers have a reputation for being homebodies,
they are amazing campers and travelers, in part because they
can quickly create the coziness of home wherever they go.

Tragedy followed when John died soon after. Thoreau was devastated by the loss. John died in his brother's arms, and in perhaps a case of empathetic pain transference, Thoreau himself developed symptoms of lockjaw for a period despite not having tetanus himself. This kind of intense compassion is a classic Cancer trait. Cancers can, in some cases, be so caught up with family and loved ones that when a family member suffers, the Cancer may feel that pain as if it is their own. There might even be an unconscious attempt to relieve the sufferer by taking on their pain. They may have a soft interior, but a crab's shell is a tough thing, and they are at once much stronger than others give them credit for and perhaps less strong than they insist on being. It is often enough simply to deal with their own emotional turmoil. It is simply too much to take on that of their loved ones.

In the mid-1830s, Thoreau struck up his legendary friendship with Ralph Waldo Emerson (Gemini). Emerson was a philosopher, abolitionist, and an established author at the center of the Transcendentalist movement. It was through Emerson that Thoreau connected with the Transcendentalists, among them Margaret Fuller (Gemini), Henry Wadsworth Longfellow (Pisces), and Amos Branson Alcott (Sagittarius). These are all, it's worth noting, double-bodied signs, or symbols represented by two physical aspects (the twins for Gemini, the two fish for Pisces, and the half man–half centaur for Sagittarius).

There was some overlap between the Transcendentalists and the Concord Writers, the latter being the province of Nathaniel Hawthorne (Cancer, see page 95). Upon meeting Thoreau through Emerson, Hawthorne was struck by how "odd looking" Thoreau was but judged him a good sort, writing, "But his ugliness is of an honest and agreeable fashion, and becomes him much better than beauty."

On July 4, 1845 (at the height of Cancer season, no less), Thoreau began the undertaking that would make him famous. As an experiment in living, he sought to survive self-sufficiently in a tiny house on the banks of Walden Pond. At a suggestion from Emerson, and with the encouragement of both Amos Branson Alcott and William Ellery Channing (both Sagittarians with the same birthday, November 29), Thoreau set out with the aim of fully integrating living and writing. It is fitting that two Sagittarians and a Gemini would encourage a Cancer to conduct an experiment in hermitage instead of doing it themselves.

Thoreau's initial writing goal was to compose an elegy to his recently deceased brother. He completed *A Week on the Concord and Merrimack Rivers* in 1848, a thoughtful remembrance of their trip together. However,

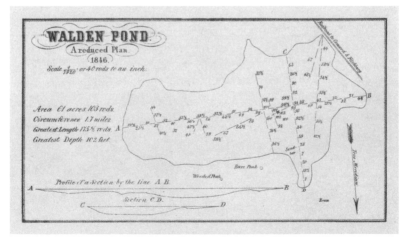

A pencil map of Walden Pond from 1846.
New York Public Library Digital Collections

it was the second book he composed while living in that house that would become his most famous work. For two years, two months, and two days, Thoreau lived at Walden. He built the little house himself, and it was important to him that it was a house rather than a shack or a writer's retreat. Cancer is the sign of the home, but Cancers also don't need much to feel at home. They

YOU MIGHT BE
A CANCER IF:
you still feel guilty about something awkward you did or said a decade ago.

take their homes with them wherever they go, which is precisely what Thoreau did. He cleared the land and planted vegetables, lived with the barest essentials, and gave himself over to nature that it might help teach him the true nature of the self. He often contemplated the evils of the world—slavery, the Native American genocide, the exploitation of the worker—and tried to better understand humankind.

Two common misconceptions tend to mark Thoreau's time at Walden. The first is that he lived as a hermit, and the second is that he cut himself off from his family—neither is true, and it is in the truth of his situation, rather, that we find much of his Cancer nature. A shy, often moody fellow with a ruminating nature, Thoreau was just as often charismatic, funny, and friendly. Cancers are often mislabeled as overly shy homebodies, when in fact they are possessed of a great love for their fellow man. They may often need to recharge in solitude, but they spring back out of their shell again to eat, laugh, and love in the company of those nearest and dearest to them. Thoreau was extremely close with his mother and sister, and especially in the wake of John's death, it would have been remarkably selfish to emotionally abandon them in the service of an experiment. Instead, he went home weekly for family dinners and partook in the affection of his family (and their desire to do his laundry for him).

That retreat at Walden is often romanticized as a kind of imaginary tableau of Thoreau living absolutely alone, deep in the woods, far from humanity, but actually his house was right on the edge of town near a busy road and beside a popular fishing hole. Instead of being a solitary hermit, he was more social than ever. His experiment was on full display for everyone to see as he lived in what scholar Laura Dassow Walls calls "ostentatious simplicity." In fact, he became something of a celebrity, and going to talk with Thoreau became a kind of trend. He spoke of himself as living as an innkeeper, with no lock on his door, and being open to all who approached him. However, although he didn't lock up his house, he did lock up his writing, which is a most fitting metaphor for Cancer—the unlocked house, open to all, but with Cancer's innermost thoughts locked up safely inside a desk drawer.

In the years that followed his drafting of *Walden*, Thoreau published *A Week on the Concord and Merrimack Rivers* (1849) to somewhat poor reviews, followed by *Walden* (1854), which was moderately successful. He would also write "Civil Disobedience" (1849), an essay that argues that sometimes it is necessary to break the law if the law is fundamentally unjust (see, for example, Thoreau's refusal to pay his taxes because he felt they were going to fund the Mexican–American War, to which he was passionately opposed). Cancers are often thought of as docile, which is a mistake that only a careless enemy would make. A cardinal sign, they are often the first moved to action and the most likely to follow through with a task they have set for themselves. They can be terribly stubborn, but when that stubbornness collides with the greater good, miraculous things can occur.

In his final years, Thoreau bounced around from working at the pencil factory to living with Emerson and the Transcendentalists, never straying far from his hometown of Concord. He never married, having fallen in love once when young, with the same woman as his brother. She refused them both but had feelings for Thoreau, and it is thought that he held a torch for her until his death by tuberculosis at the age of forty-four.

CASE STUDY #2: ANN RADCLIFFE

If Horace Walpole (Libra, see page 152) is considered the father of Gothic literature, then Ann Radcliffe is not only its mother but the uncles, aunts, and friendly neighbors that collectively work together to raise the child. Walpole may have initiated the genre with his groundbreakingly bizarre *The Castle of Otranto* (1764), but it was Radcliffe with her massive tomes and her quiet attention to form that created the foundations of the genre as we know it today. Leave it to a Cancer to unobtrusively create, gestate, and nurture a genre that at its core is about secrets and hidden things.

Born in 1764 in London to a haberdasher and his wife, Radcliffe and her family moved to Bath when she was eight, where her father ran a china shop. By all accounts, Radcliffe was a rather shy child. There is often a sense of mystery that surrounds Cancers—not the overt mystery of a Scorpio or the tenebrous mystery of a Capricorn (Cancer's opposite sign), but a quiet kind of mystery that often accompanies a deeply private person. The irony, of course, is that privacy itself often draws a prying kind of focus.

Not much is known about Radcliffe's personal life, and the few early biographies on the subject were filled with misinformation that continued to be repeated until the task of accurately unearthing her life essentially led to a hall of mirrors. What's funny is that, of all the signs, Cancer is the most associated with memory, and yet collectively we have almost no memory of Radcliffe. When a crab is intent on hiding in its shell, it's desperately hard to retrieve. Christina Rossetti (Sagittarius) apparently attempted a biography at one point but was unable to uncover enough relevant information to proceed. You can be certain that if a Sagittarius can't find what they're after, it means it's hard to find.

We do know that Radcliffe was happily married to an editor named William Radcliffe who served as a key supporter of her writing. Initially, Radcliffe wrote to entertain herself, and William delighted in the tales, which she would often read to him upon his return from work each day. Although she embodied the Cancer stereotype of a shy homebody, Radcliffe wrote of faraway places and terrifying men. From the confines of her comfortable lifestyle and supportive marriage, she imagined great drafty castles and brigands intent on absconding with innocent girls' virtue. It is perhaps this contrast that made Radcliffe so adept at creating the scary-yet-cozy vibe that is integral to the genre of Gothic literature.

In part, this is because of the debt that the Gothic novel owes to the sentimental novel. Whereas Walpole may have been attempting to subvert the sentimental novel, Radcliffe was able to successfully incorporate some of its most popular tropes. The typical sentimental novel relied heavily on emotion. Often located within the domestic sphere and meant to appeal to female readers, the works tended to offer a Manichean view of the world, with the good, domestically confined protagonist being acted upon by an evil, external societal force. It was then up to the heroine to refuse the iniquitous influence in favor of divinity and freedom from sin. Novels like *Pamela; or, Virtue Rewarded* (1740) and *Clarissa; or, the History of a Young Lady* (1748), both by Samuel Richardson (Leo), had been hugely popular in their time, and Radcliffe drew on some of that sentimental texture to create her Gothic landscapes.

Classically, Gothic fiction is a heroine-focused genre that derives its appeal from a pleasantly frightening atmosphere and tone. Often situated in dramatic settings, such as castles beset by inclement weather, Gothic novels are reliant on a specific kind of terror that emphasizes fear of the unknown and a preoccupation with death. Yet there is an attractiveness to the death and decay so pervasive in the Gothic. This enjoyable kind of terror was first discussed by noted author and critic Anna Laetitia Barbauld (née Aikin), who wrote of it, "The apparent delight with which we dwell upon objects of pure terror, where our moral feelings are not in the least concerned, and no passion seems to be excited but the depressing one of fear, is a paradox of the heart."

Radcliffe managed this pleasing terror in part because she was so intent on giving the reader what they wanted. She mixed the terrifying with the sublime and the titillating with the comforting with such skill that she inspired a devoted (mostly female) readership and became hugely popular in her time. Her most successful novel, and the novel perhaps most emblematic of the Gothic genre to this day, is *The Mysteries of Udolpho* (1794). The story of an orphaned young woman imprisoned in a moldering castle by a villainous scoundrel who also happens to be her uncle by marriage contains everything Gothic readers hungered for—thrilling mysteries, exotically gloomy locales, hints of taboo relations, and, of course, last-minute escapes. Radcliffe essentially invented the classic *Scooby-Doo* plot in which what seems to be an unequivocally supernatural, threatening force is neatly explained away at the conclusion of the story, at which point the heroine is whisked to safety.

CUTE VINTAGE BABY NAMES
from ANN RADCLIFFE NOVELS

Adeline	Clara	Ellena	Julia
Annette	Cornelia	Emilia	Louisa
Caterina	Dorothée	Emily	Matilda

Despite her popularity and success (she was the highest-paid author of her time), Radcliffe became reclusive later in life. Rumors swirled about her. Was she in ill health? Perhaps she was afflicted with some mysterious disease, or had she, like some tertiary Gothic character, gone mad? Or was she simply giving in to her Cancer nature and staying at home because it was quiet and that's what she preferred? She died in 1823 of what was most likely an upper respiratory infection, but she left behind a legacy that would set the course for a hybrid genre still popular today.

CASE STUDY #3: MATTHEW "MONK" LEWIS

If Radcliffe imbued the Gothic genre with its pleasant terror, then Matthew "Monk" Lewis is responsible for creating its seedy underbelly. Born to a wealthy government official and a doting, artistically inclined mother, Lewis's writing exemplifies some of the more quietly sinister aspects of the sign of Cancer. Unlike a Scorpio or an Aquarius, though, Cancers often keep that darker side on the margins, hinting at it rather than living it and, in Matthew Lewis's case, writing about it.

Lewis earned bachelor's and master's degrees from Oxford and was a prolific translator. Like many people with strong Cancer placements, Lewis was incredibly close with his mother, writing in large part to earn money for her after she separated from his father. A gifted linguist, having studied German from a young age, he translated works by Kleist (Libra), Schiller (Scorpio), and Goethe (Virgo), among others.

At nineteen, encouraged by his mother to write, he penned what is perhaps the most infamous example of the Gothic novel. Composed in a sensationalistic style and published anonymously, *The Monk* (1796) dealt explicitly with the most scandalous topics. Every possible taboo subject was treated in sparkling detail. *The Monk* contains, among other things, a lecherous oversexed monk, a pregnant demonic nun, a man who accidentally elopes with a bloody ghost nun, rape, pacts with the devil, dead babies, and the Inquisition. The literary establishment didn't quite know what to make of it. Among Lewis's harshest critics was none other than Ann Radcliffe, who was repulsed by the deleterious nature of *The Monk*. She would go on to write a short piece expressing her thoughts on the difference between terror and horror, arguing that "Terror and Horror are so far opposite that the first expands the soul, and awakens the faculties to a high degree of life; the other contracts, freezes and nearly annihilates them."

Although critics were horrified, the general public was enamored, and Lewis, who eventually exposed himself as the author, counted both the Marquis de Sade (Gemini) and the notorious Lord Byron (Aquarius, see "A Note on Cusp Figures," page 274) among his fans. He went on to become friends with Byron and even visited him, Polidori, and the Shelleys on the shores of Lake Geneva during the same summer when they held their famous ghost story competition.

Lewis went on to write another novel and a few collections of work as well as several plays, one of which, *The Captive* (1803), contained so much onstage violence that it was shut down midway through the first performance and was never performed again during Lewis's lifetime. Thought to be inspired by *The Wrongs of Woman, or Maria* by Mary Wollstonecraft (Taurus, see page 44), *The Captive* contains almost no dialogue and (as far as scholars have gleaned) the action consists only of a woman being imprisoned and tortured onstage for what was meant to be several hours. Although there is no indication that Lewis himself was violent or abusive, his work concentrated on violence, sadism, and the more malevolent aspects of human nature almost to a singular degree. Cancers' insistence on excavating collective sin can often be uncomfortable to observe.

Although *The Monk* isn't the most pleasant of reads, Lewis's importance must not be discounted. His work influenced some of the most famous Western writers of all time, from Charlotte Brontë (Taurus, see page 51) to Charles Dickens (Aquarius, see page 245) and Victor Hugo (Pisces), from Coleridge (Libra, see page 164) to Flaubert (Sagittarius) to Kleist (Libra) and both Mary (Virgo, see page 131) and Percy Bysshe (Leo, see page 106) Shelley.

Lewis never married, instead living the carefree life of the bon vivant, socializing and serving as a member of the House of Commons, where he approached his governance with a laissez-faire attitude at best. He died of yellow fever at the age of forty-two. Befitting his watery sign, he was buried at sea.

CODA: NATHANIEL HAWTHORNE

If Cancers are known for their penchant to hide in their shells, they are often equally adept at drawing other hidden things into the light. A descendant of William Hathorne, a notoriously harsh judge who presided over the Salem witch trials, Nathaniel Hawthorne was practically obsessed with excavating the sins of his forefathers. He added the *W* to his last name to distance himself from his ancestor and wrote with an almost singular focus about the dark side of Puritan excess. After college, he moved back home to live with his mother and sister, which he did for more than a decade, writing and honing his craft. On July 9, 1842, he married Sophia Peabody (Virgo), a Transcendentalist painter.

Cancer is the place of a hidden kind of darkness, the kind that throbs just below the surface in moist soil and mossy crevices. Hawthorne's writing was deeply allegorical, infused with representations of sin and salvation, of deep dark forests and hidden machinations. In "Young Goodman Brown" (1835), the narrator discovers that his entire town has been engaged in secret activities right under his nose and finds himself questioning the very nature of faith. In "Egotism; or, the Bosom Serpent" (1843), a man whose sin has become corporeal (a serpent residing in his bosom) insists on pointing out the invisible serpents that reside in his neighbors' chests.

But while much of his work deals with Cancer themes, in *The Scarlet Letter* (1850) we find them expressed most clearly. It is in this book that the Cancer adulation of motherhood and the ability to turn an

That Cancer writer you meet may be a chummy bro in person.
Just don't be surprised if his work in progress contains the darkest shit you've ever seen.

unflinching eye toward the darker aspects of the human psyche collide. The story of a pregnant woman punished as an adulterer, forced to wear a red *A* pinned to her chest, and shunned from her village, *The Scarlet Letter* dives deep into motherhood, pregnancy, hidden motives, and secrecy. The main character, Hester Prynne, is forced to live like a hermit on the edge of town, and yet it is in exile that she finds not only her solace but a deep sense of peace. With this book, Hawthorne highlights how much more difficult it is for the thinking person to live within the suffocating confines of a draconian system premised on hypocrisy than it is to subsist on one's own. In Hester Prynne we find hints of Thoreau and his Walden. Although Hawthorne was dealing with lofty themes that transcend astrological compartmentalization, it's still rather easy to see in his writing the Cancer introvert, simply wishing to be left alone.

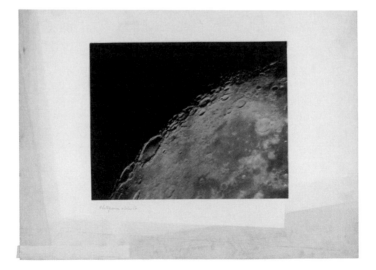

NOTES FOR WRITERS WITH OTHER CANCER PLACEMENTS

WRITER'S CORNER

POSITIVE ASPECTS

You have incredible empathy and an almost ferocious love for your friends and family. Use these gifts to deeply move your readers.

NEGATIVE ASPECTS

Your moodiness can be tremendous for your writing, but if you're bringing too much pathos to what should be a light piece, take a break, get some air, and clear your head.

WRITER BEWARE

You can be overly sensitive, so you may want to be careful about the people with whom you share your work. Make sure you can handle their feedback before you ask for it.

CANCER MOON: You are extremely sensitive and conflict-avoidant, but just because you dislike conflict in your life doesn't mean you don't need some on the page. Work on raising the stakes in your writing and possibly introducing some—you guessed it—conflict. Privacy is important to you, so you tend to keep your writing to yourself. Put yourself out there. There is an audience for your writing. You just have to let them find you.

CANCER RISING: You can be quite gifted at understanding what motivates people. You are adaptable, endowed with a tremendous imagination, and extremely sensitive to the emotions of others. As such, you populate your writing with believable characters and your work is apt to appeal to a wide audience. However, because you tend to be a little moody, you don't care much about the spotlight. Genius seldom needs external light sources to shine.

MERCURY IN CANCER: As a writer, you are deeply intuitive and may even have a touch of the psychic in you. This means you can trust your writerly instincts. Whether that comes down to word choice, narrative style, or plot arcs, follow your intuition wherever it may take you.

VENUS IN CANCER: You are made up of equal parts blind romanticism and quiet practicality. In your writing this means that you could be the next Jane Austen. No matter your preferred genre, consider adding some romance to your work. You may be much more adept at writing about the subject than you realize.

MARS IN CANCER: As a writer, you have a magnificent capacity for endurance. Although you are loath to call attention to how much you keep at a task, your dogged persistence is bound to be your key to success. Follow that quietly determined voice that tells you to keep going, whether that means pushing ahead with that novel that seems to never end or submitting your work to that journal one more time. We know you've got what it takes.

TRY THIS!

+ WRITE a poem beneath the light of the full moon.

+ DISAPPEAR from society for a day or two. Whether that means finding your own personal Walden or simply limiting your internet access, discover what comes to life when you allow your innermost voices to rise to the surface.

+ TAKE a walk in nature. Clear your mind. Write about a secret.

READER'S CORNER:
COMPATIBILITY CHART

Which Cancer-composed book is most likely to appeal to you? It depends on your sign. Look for your match below. And don't forget to look at your rising and Moon signs if you know those.

SIGN	CLASSIC	MODERN
ARIES	ANNA AKHMATOVA, *The Complete Poems*	OCTAVIA BUTLER, *Kindred*
TAURUS	ALICE DUNBAR-NELSON, *The Goodness of St. Rocque*	ELIZABETH GILBERT, *Big Magic: Creative Living Beyond Fear*
GEMINI	FRANZ KAFKA, *The Metamorphosis*	TEJU COLE, *Open City*
CANCER	ANN RADCLIFFE, *The Romance of the Forest*	TONY KUSHNER, *Angels in America*
LEO	WILLIAM MAKEPEACE THACKERAY, *Vanity Fair*	JHUMPA LAHIRI, *Interpreter of Maladies*
VIRGO	HART CRANE, *Complete Poems and Selected Letters*	ALICE MUNRO, *My Best Stories*

SIGN	CLASSIC	MODERN
LIBRA	NATHANIEL HAWTHORNE, *The Scarlet Letter*	LEV GROSSMAN, *The Magicians*
SCORPIO	MATTHEW LEWIS, *The Monk*	REBECCA SOLNIT, *Orwell's Roses*
SAGITTARIUS	HENRY DAVID THOREAU, *Walden*	CORMAC MCCARTHY, *The Road*
CAPRICORN	PABLO NERUDA, *Twenty Love Poems and A Song of Despair*	DAN BROWN, *The Da Vinci Code*
AQUARIUS	JACQUES DERRIDA, *Writing and Difference*	LOUISE PENNY, *Still Life*
PISCES	HELEN KELLER, *The Story of My Life*	WOLE SOYINKA, *Death and the King's Horsemen*

✦ **LEO** ✦

LEO

THE **EXTRA** WRITER

I WOULD PREFER NOT TO.

—Herman Melville

LEO 101

Leos are born with an inherent understanding of their own greatness. Although it can seem they are driven by a singular focus on the self, quite the opposite is often true. Their self-confidence imbues them with a sense that they should be in charge of something—usually a group of some kind—and are therefore responsible for that thing. If a Leo seems to take charge and assume responsibility, declaring themself the leader, it isn't necessarily because they want to be the leader, but rather because they feel a responsibility for the well-being and success of the group at large. This can sometimes be a bit much for members of the group who don't necessarily want or need a leader, but to ascribe a tyrannical solipsism to a Leo is to miss half the story.

Leos are the royalty of the zodiac and they know it. But being born with a scepter in one's hand can be a daunting enterprise; if you start out at the top, there is nowhere to go but down. This inborn sense of precariousness gives Leo a secret undercurrent of anxiety. Perhaps because they are ruled by the Sun, Leos have a sense of their rightful heliocentric position at the center of things, whether that be a family, a community, or a social movement. They are tormented by a vague sense that if they aren't at the center, it will all inevitably descend into chaos and destruction. It is up to them to keep it all together.

SIGN OVERVIEW

SYMBOL:
The Lion

ELEMENT: Fire

QUALITY: Fixed

HOUSE RULED:
5th (Romance, Creativity, Children)

PLANETARY RULER:
The Sun

POSITIVE TRAITS:
Charismatic, Generous, Noble

NEGATIVE TRAITS:
Self-Focused, Arrogant, Tyrannical

Fame is often a transient way of achieving this centrality and relieving Leo's anxiety. However, this drive toward fame is often grounded in a desire to exist beyond their own mortality, which can infuse the sign with a preternatural bravery. Their focus on the long term (we're talking immortality here) can make the here and now seem less important in the larger scheme of things and can lead to acts of utter heroism. It can also make them horridly self-centered and egotistical, but with Leo, one must learn to take the good with the bad.

Leo rules the 5th House of romance, creativity, and children. In fact, more than probably any other sign, Leos tend to get along well with children. Leos possess a playful, childlike quality and a genuine enthusiasm for life that puts the rest of the zodiac to shame. They can also be extremely generous. In fact, Leo's generosity is an aspect of their character that often gets overlooked. They want every member of their pride to succeed, and when needed, they will make themselves available at the drop of a hat.

Leos may seem like tyrannical authoritarians, but in reality, they are the shoulder to cry on and the exact person to go to if you need encouragement or someone to pick you up when you are at your lowest point. As long as you can handle some charmingly self-focused Leo lore, they will stay by your side for literally as long as you can listen to them talk about themselves. With a helpful dose of Leo's Sun, you'll be able to manage any rough patch the universe might throw at you. Plus, if you don't feel better soon, you won't get to see Leo's one-person show, performed every night at the center of the town square. And you wouldn't want to miss that, now would you?

THE LEO WRITER:
A LITERARY HISTORY

Leo writers are hard to miss. They live loudly, they rebel against authority, and they often explode everything around them while writing similarly explosive prose. Percy Bysshe Shelley wrote beautiful poetry while causing mayhem and destruction everywhere he went. Emily Brontë wrote a novel of shockingly excessive emotion, the popularity of which never seems to fade. Herman Melville chased the literary relevance he will never know he ultimately achieved, and Wallace Thurman used his charismatic brilliance to help create one of the most incandescent literary movements of all time.

CASE STUDY #1: PERCY BYSSHE SHELLEY

Sometimes Leos have a problem with authority. We'll just come right out and say it. Some Leos know instinctively how to become an authority, so they don't actually have much to rebel against, but others fight so hard against authority that it can make their lives rather difficult. Such was the case with Percy Bysshe Shelley. Whether that authority was familial, moral, or governmental, Shelley actively thumbed his nose at it.

Born into wealth as the son of a prominent politician, Shelley had what was most likely a remarkably pleasant childhood, complete with lots of land to wander and lots of adoring female relatives to lavish affection on him. However, almost as soon as he was sent off to school, Shelley had a difficult time of it. He responded poorly to authority and with heated animus to bullying, which proved something of a vicious cycle. His temper was so explosive that the bullies often got exactly the results they wanted from him, which only served to further his torment. It was around this time that Shelley started blowing things up. Leos love a good explosion, and in their more emotional moments nothing soothes as much as the act of causing a sudden violent conflagration. Leos almost always immediately regret that destruction, but the outburst itself is a form of catharsis for this highly dramatic sign.

Shelley's love of explosions coupled nicely with his interest in science, and throughout his school days he was given to setting up science labs in his living quarters in which he would experiment with all manner of volatile materials. Shelley was similarly inflammatory in his political beliefs. He was a vegetarian, and under the influence of Thomas Jefferson Hogg (Gemini), whom he met at Oxford, he became an outspoken atheist at a time when that could get you into a fair amount of trouble. When he and Hogg were eventually expelled from Oxford because of a scandalizing pamphlet they coauthored, Shelley went on to fight with his father and to elope with Harriet Westbrook (Leo), a student at his sisters' boarding school, whom it seems he was intent on rescuing despite possibly having manufactured the circumstances from which she needed to be rescued. Both fathers cut off their Leo progeny, and for a while, the couple lived together in a professed utopian experiment that likely included a healthy dose of polyamory.

Estranged from his father and lacking an authority figure against whom to rebel, Shelley devoted himself to the mentorship of author and philosopher William Godwin (Pisces), before exploding that relationship by running off with his sixteen-year-old daughter, Mary (Virgo, see page 131), and taking her stepsister, Claire Clairmont (Taurus), with them. Scandal ensued and would follow Shelley for the rest of his life; his first wife, Harriet, committed suicide and Mary lost several children to miscarriages and early deaths, all while Shelley developed a series of infatuations with (often married) women. He believed in free love and most likely encouraged Mary to live similarly, though there is little evidence that this was actually her choice. Sometimes a Leo's generosity can look a lot like selfishness.

In 1816, Shelley became friends with Lord Byron (Aquarius, see "A Note on Cusp Figures," page 274), and together with their small, avant-garde coterie, they lived in active defiance of convention. Byron fathered a child with Claire Clairmont, with whom Shelley most likely had an affair as well. There were secret children, adopted children, abandoned children, and neglected children left in the wake of this destructive alliance. Meanwhile, as Lord Byron skyrocketed to fame, Shelley was unable to attain equivalent notoriety, which must have been difficult for a Leo. It's hard to be the center of things when Lord Byron is around. It just is. If you are a Leo and you meet a Lord Byron, run in the other direction lest your fame be eclipsed and your ego dealt a mighty blow.

Throughout his life, Shelley wrote essays, fiction, political tracts, and some of the finest poems ever written, but during his own lifetime he never achieved a modicum of Byron's fame. However, his talent as a poet is unquestionable. His poems are often imbued with a Leo's appreciation for timelessness and antiquity such as can be observed in "Ozymandias," a meditation on greatness destined for destruction, or "Adonais," an emotional elegy he composed upon Keats's (Scorpio) untimely death.

The awful shadow of some unseen Power /
Floats though unseen among us

—PERCY BYSSHE SHELLEY, "HYMN TO INTELLECTUAL BEAUTY"

A classic Leo, Shelley was reckless, and in 1822 he died at sea with Edward Williams (Taurus) in a boat that was possibly not seaworthy and which the men on board were incapable of handling. It is said that when his body washed up onshore, his pocket held a volume of Keats's poetry, in what can perhaps be seen as a final Leonine gesture of excessive sentimentality. He was only twenty-nine years old when he succumbed to that ultimate natural authority—the sea.

CASE STUDY #2: WALLACE THURMAN

Although Wallace Thurman may not be the first name that comes to mind when you think of the Harlem Renaissance, according to his contemporaries, he was one of the most important and most radical figures of his day. Dorothy West (Gemini) went so far as to call him the movement's "most symbolic figure." Rakishly handsome and in possession of a typically Leonine proclivity for sparking controversy, during his short life Wallace Thurman took the literary world by storm. He wrote as decadently as he lived, thumbed his nose at every establishment he could find, and infused his work with a deliciously satirical eye that was far ahead of his time.

Born in 1902 in Salt Lake City, Utah, Thurman was a sickly child with a heart problem who was forced to miss significant amounts of school in his early days. His father left when he was only a month old, and in subsequent years, Thurman moved around a great deal, from Boise to Chicago to Omaha, and even back to Salt Lake City at one point to live with his grandmother.

Thurman read prodigiously and was enamored with the writing of Plato, Goethe (Virgo), and Dostoevsky (Scorpio). He also wrote from a young age, composing his first novel at the age of ten. After graduating from high school, Thurman studied at the University of Utah and the University of Southern California, taking premed and journalism courses, respectively. Thurman then moved to Harlem, where he not only settled into the flourishing artistic and cultural scene afoot, but also quickly became the very center of it. Not all Leos necessarily want to be at the center of a historic movement, but it never hurts to have one there. Along with serving on the staff of several literary magazines, Thurman published widely, including in the *Independent*, the *New Republic*, the *New York Evening Post*, *American Monthly*, the *Greenwich Village Quill*, and the *New York Times*.

An incisive and satirical critic, he quickly made a name for himself and established friendships with other critics noted for their acerbic wit, such as Dorothy Parker, a fellow Leo, with whom he corresponded regularly. His closest friendship, however, seems to have been with famed poet Langston Hughes (Aquarius), with whom he and Arna Bontemps (Libra) started the magazine *Fire!!*. Astrologically, a friendship between a Leo like Thurman and an Aquarius like Hughes makes for an interesting case study because those two signs sit across from each other on the zodiac, meaning each possesses qualities that the other lacks. Sometimes these relationships can cause friction, but ideally they bring out the best in each other, as seems to have been the case with Thurman and Hughes.

Thurman is perhaps best remembered for *The Blacker the Berry* (1929), a novel that is notable both for its unflinching depiction of racism and colorism and for its early focus on what has since been termed *misogynoir*—the idea that Black women face a very specific doubling bias that includes a complex interplay of racism and sexism. Thurman also collaborated on two plays and a novel with fellow writer William Jourdan Rapp (Gemini). Collaboration isn't the first word that comes to mind in relation to Leos, but when a Leo finds someone they can work with, no other sign is happier to be able to finally let go of some of their burden—a genial Gemini who appreciates Leos' wit is a positive match if ever there was one.

Although he was an immensely talented writer, being an artist was only one aspect of Thurman's influential personality. A classic Leo,

Thurman looked out for his pride, supporting his fellow authors and championing avant-garde work. He insisted on an ethos of art for art's sake, a sensibility that often put him in direct conflict with some of the Harlem Renaissance's most esteemed figures, who felt that art (and art by Black artists, in particular) should always serve a political end.

Notably, Thurman clashed with the eminent Alain Locke (Virgo). Some scholars maintain that Thurman and Locke engaged in a rivalry for the center of the movement; in *The Making of the New Negro* (2011), author Anna Pochmara claims this stemmed "not only from personal ambition but from the glaring disparity in their visions of the artistic movement, race relations, the black collective subject, and authorship." Locke asserted that Black artists needed to be pragmatic and politically engaged, but Thurman was cynical about this idea and made a case for privileging the individual and for radicalism in art without a need for political relevance. Thurman was also slyly critical of the idea of the movement itself, often referring to the Harlem Renaissance as "so-called" and "well-advertised."

If there ever was a quintessentially Leo book, it almost certainly is Thurman's *Infants of the Spring* (1932). Often considered both a satire and a celebration of the Harlem Renaissance, it has also been called an elegy to the era. Published at the tail end of the artistic movement, it captures both the ecstatic beating heart of the time as well as the sense of its impending dissipation into the Great Depression.

Populated with thinly veiled caricatures of real Harlem Renaissance figures (Locke makes an appearance, as do W. E. B. Du Bois, Langston Hughes, and Zora Neale Hurston, among others), *Infants of the Spring* makes use of Thurman's centrality to the movement. Although he has never been properly integrated into the canon (or even widely acknowledged as a central figure of the Harlem Renaissance), in reality, Thurman was the social center of the movement, with the house he rented serving as its headquarters. His house (on which Thurman and Zora Neale Hurston deliberately bestowed an offensive name) hosted literary salons and rent parties, and quickly became the spectacular nexus of the Harlem Renaissance. It is in and around a fictionalized version of this house that *Infants of the Spring* takes place.

Exploring themes of racial prejudice, sexual liberation, and gender inequality, the novel also expresses Thurman's refusal to prioritize racial politics over his own personal identity. In Raymond (a stand-in for Thurman) we have an infectiously charismatic main character who lives life to its fullest and refuses to conform to anyone's standards but his own. Upon meeting a visiting white man from Denmark, Raymond welcomes him to his lavish dwellings, offering him a highball and decrying the kinds of white guests to whom a mutual friend typically subjects him, including "caponized radicals, lady versifiers who gush all over the place . . . and others of the same dogassed ilk."

Thurman refused to restrict his exquisite lampooning to his fiction, however. He was a critic of the first rate, and in his private correspondences he was the very picture of Leonine hilarity. Take this letter he wrote to Langston Hughes, in which he jokingly disparages nearly every important writer of the time (except for Jean Toomer):

Found [McKay's] *Banjo* turgid and tiresome. *Passing* [by Nella Larsen] possessed of the same faults as [her] *Quicksand. Rope and Faggot* [by Walter White] is good for a library reference. Nella Larsen can write, but oh my god she knows so little how to invest her characters with any lifelike possibilities. They always outrage the reader, not naturally as people have a way of doing in real life, but artificially like ill-managed puppets. Claude [McKay] I believe has shot his blot. Jessie Fauset should be taken to Philadelphia and cremated. You should write a book. Countee [Cullen] should be castrated and taken to Persia as the Shah's eunuch. Jean Toomer should be enshrined as a genius and immortal and he should also publish his new book about which gossip is raving. Bud [Rudolph] Fisher should stick to short stories. Zora [Hurston] should learn craftsmanship and surprise the world and outstrip her contemporaries as well. Bruce [Nugent] should be spanked, put in a monastery and made to concentrate on writing. Gwennie [Gwendolyn Bennett] should stick to what she is doing. Aaron [Douglas] needs a change of scenery and a psychic shock. Eric [Walrond] ought to finish the *Big Ditch* [later *Tropic Death*] or destroy it. I should commit suicide.

There has perhaps never been a more Leo paragraph written in the history of humankind.

The transition from the 1920s to the 1930s saw Thurman's star on the rise and gave no indication that it would fall anytime soon. He and Rapp had found tremendous success on Broadway with their play *Harlem* (1929), and Thurman had just transitioned to writing screenplays in Hollywood. Tragically, in 1934 he fell ill with tuberculosis and died a scant six months later at the age of thirty-two. On December 26, 1934, the Harlem Renaissance lost one of its most radical geniuses, and the world lost a true Leo king.

CASE STUDY #3: HERMAN MELVILLE

Herman Melville is an outsized figure who embodied as much of the Leo nature in his life as he did in his fiction. Although he is responsible for penning what has long been considered one of the greatest novels of all time (*Moby-Dick*, 1851), he also died in near obscurity and with very little money to his name. Like his great white whale, he surged through life, making waves wherever he went.

Melville was born into great opulence and a warm and doting family. The third of eight children, initially he received a top-notch education at New York Male High School, which he attended with his brother. However, his life changed dramatically when, in 1831, his father suddenly died. The loss was emotionally excruciating for Melville, and practically overnight his family went from wealthy to nearly destitute. Melville was forced to quit school. At the age of twenty, he got a low-level job on a whaling ship and took to sea. The next few years of his life were marked by adventure that would inspire much of his literary work.

Like many Leos, Melville had a problem with authority and a desire to forge his own route. This penchant was on full display throughout his sea years, during which he jumped ship with a crewmate, lived in the Marquesas, took up with another ship, assisted with a mutiny, was jailed in Tahiti, escaped, and lived as an aimless outlaw in Polynesia for two years. This is Leo living writ large. What's more, upon his return home, he had tales enough to entertain his friends and family for years to come. His stories were so enthralling, in fact, that those same friends and family encouraged him to write them down. Eventually he did just that, publishing *Typee* (1846) and *Omoo* (1847) as lightly fictionalized travel memoirs. The books were an almost-immediate success and served to launch Melville's literary career.

In 1850, Melville met Nathaniel Hawthorne (Cancer, see page 95), and in him he found a mentor, a father figure, and a friend. The two became very close, often drinking and smoking together while talking for hours, each man impressed by the other's intellectual abilities and artistic temperament. Melville's adoration for him (which some contend may have been romantic) inspired him to dedicate *Moby-Dick* to Hawthorne.

The death of Melville's father had a persistent influence on the author. The Sun rules Leo and typifies the paternal influence. For some Leos this can mean a focus on the father as the ultimate authority to overthrow. But Melville was granted no father to overthrow, so he grappled with paternity in his fiction instead. Absent fathers sprint through Melville's work, their desertion leaving a swath of paternal proxies and searching young men whose guidebooks and portraits and maritime journeys never seem to lead them to the fathers with whom they wish to reunite. This paternal absence is probably most overt in *Pierre: or, The Ambiguities* (1852), a novel in which the entire plot hinges on a missing father.

However, it is in *Moby-Dick* that we observe the author's Leonine fascination with the mythic and the immortal. The story of a sea voyage and the search for an enormous white whale (a mission that drives its captain mad), *Moby-Dick* is stylistically complicated and far ahead of its time. It's a behemoth of a book with an almost postmodern focus on whaling-industry-related minutiae. Its narrative is anything but linear and its depictions of maritime life anything but heroic. Its ambition, however, was Leo to the extreme.

Despite that effulgent ambitious-ness, though, *Moby-Dick* proved to be a disaster for Melville; rather than being the apex of his career, it became the signpost of his impending failure. Critics disliked the book, and its sales were extremely poor. Not long after its publication, Melville also became estranged from Hawthorne. The exact nature of their split remains a mystery, but astrologically speaking, a live-out-loud Leo who seemed intent on digesting every possible human experience may simply have been too much for our mysterious Cancer, a sign prone to holding their emotional cards close to

Both jaws, like enormous shears, bit the craft completely in twain.

New York Public Library Digital Collections

their chest. Whatever the reason behind their estrangement, this once-glorious friendship in which they discussed "the universe with a bottle of brandy & cigars" came to a regrettable end, though it's clear that Melville maintained at least a quiet devotion to Hawthorne. It is widely supposed that Melville's poem "Monody" (1891) is a eulogy of Hawthorne:

> To have known him, to have loved him
> After loneness long;
> And then to be estranged in life,
> And neither in the wrong;
> And now for death to set his seal—
> Ease me, a little ease, my song!
> By wintry hills his hermit-mound
> The sheeted snow-drifts drape,
> And houseless there the snow-bird flits
> Beneath the fir-trees' crape:
> Glazed now with ice the cloistral vine
> That hid the shyest grape.

After the critical and financial failure of *Moby-Dick*, and feeling the pressure of the market, Melville looked to popular fiction as a means of escape from the critical quagmire in which he found himself. At the time, the success of sentimental novels, or domestic fiction, was sweeping the nation. The extreme commercial and financial success of Susan Warner's (Cancer) *The Wide, Wide World* (1850) shifted the popular imagination toward a new, female-authored, female-focused bildungsroman in which modern domesticity was front and center. There was no question that the public had a taste for this new, perhaps less artistically focused kind of book. Indeed, the prime example of the genre, *The Lamplighter* (1854) by Maria Susanna Cummins, sold four times as many copies during its first month of publication as Hawthorne's *The Scarlet Letter* sold during his lifetime. This dissonance between high art and economically viable work necessarily created frustration for writers like Hawthorne and Melville who were all but ignored in favor of what they perceived to be less-literary works. In a letter to his editor, William D. Ticknor, in January 1855, Hawthorne wrote,

> America is now wholly given over to a damned mob of scribbling women, and I should have no chance of success while the public taste is occupied with their trash—and should be ashamed of myself if I did succeed. What is the mystery of these innumerable editions of the "Lamplighter," and other books neither better nor worse?—worse they could not be, and better they need not be, when they sell by the 100,000.

It was in an effort to ride this popular, sentimental wave that Melville composed *Pierre: or, The Ambiguities*. Part sentimental, part Gothic, *Pierre* is a wild ride that dares to ask the question: What if you took *Wuthering Heights*, made it weirder, added some ickiness and incest, some polyamorous living situations, and an angry screed about the publishing industry, and then composed it all in a faux sentimental/Gothic style that manages to hit both notes falsely and stick neither landing? The result is sort of a beautiful disaster of a book that is tremendous fun to read, but for which the market of 1852 was not exactly prepared. It was declared an unequivocal failure.

READING LIST:
Beautiful Disaster Books

1. HENRY VON OFTERDINGEN: A ROMANCE by Novalis (Taurus)

2. CONFESSIONS OF AN ENGLISH OPIUM-EATER by Thomas De Quincey (Leo)

3. PIERRE: OR, THE AMBIGUITIES by Herman Melville (Leo)

4. VISIONS OF CODY by Jack Kerouac (Pisces)

5. THE GARDEN OF EDEN by Ernest Hemingway (Cancer)

Eventually, Melville was dropped by his publisher and would never write professionally again. Although he did a brief stint on the speaking circuit (Leos love an audience) and continued to write poetry, he ultimately became a customs inspector, working in anonymity until his death. He would die never having any idea of the massive literary influence his books, and *Moby-Dick* in particular, would have. It wasn't until 1919, twenty-eight years after his death, that his magnum opus would receive the attention it was due. An essay by Carl Van Doren (Virgo) and a biography by D. H. Lawrence (Virgo) would shine a light on just how narratively interesting and critically important the book is. Their attention helped Melville claim his proper place among literary greats, posthumously though that reclamation might have been. Leave it to a couple of Virgos to make sense of a riotous Leo.

CODA: EMILY BRONTË

While some Leo writers may demand a spotlight, Emily Brontë is a much more mysterious character, one who is almost impossible to know except through her writing. As one of the three famous Brontë sisters, Emily's biography has been shaped by her sister Charlotte (Taurus, see page 51) and, to an extent, by Charlotte's biographer Elizabeth Gaskell (Libra). For more than a century, the popular view of Emily Brontë has been that of a strange, spooky sister given to violent outbursts and possibly even madness. More recently, this vision of Emily has been significantly challenged, and scholars are still trying to piece together what might have been the truth of Emily's character.

What we do know of the author is that she was born in Yorkshire, England, the fifth of six children. Not long after her birth, the family moved to Haworth, where her father took a position as a curate. Her mother died when she was three. Soon after, her older sisters, Maria (Taurus), Elizabeth (Aquarius), and Charlotte, were sent away to school, and Emily would eventually join them for a short while. Tragedy struck at the school and the two eldest sisters died, possibly of typhus, possibly of tuberculosis.

No doubt burdened by grief, Emily, at home with her brother, Branwell (Cancer), and her sisters Charlotte and Anne (Capricorn), lost herself in imaginary play in the form of creative writing. At first the group created stories together, but eventually there was a split, with the older Charlotte and Branwell working together and the younger Emily and Anne making up a fantasy world they called Gondal, populated with writers who served as kinds of demigods.

In adulthood, Emily worked outside the home briefly as a teacher, but the appointment was cut short by illness and she soon returned home, where she took to running the house for her father. Although one doesn't typically associate Leo with the domestic sphere, it is very much like a Leo to be in charge of something, and for a woman in the 1800s, being in charge of running a house perhaps provided a Leo with the necessary outlet for her inborn regality. In addition to cooking and cleaning house, Emily was also in charge of shooting and cleaning the family's pistol, which is a Leonine image if there ever was one. (Remember, Leos love to explode things.)

Cognizant of the prejudice with which female writers were often received, the sisters decided to take on pseudonyms, publishing their first collection of poems as Acton, Ellis, and Currer Bell to significant acclaim. Although their careers were going well, their perpetually tragic home life remained bleak. Branwell, once the happy center of the siblings, had descended into severe depression and alcoholism. Perhaps under this shadow, the sisters returned to writing as an outlet, and in the space of a few years they wrote three of the most influential novels of the nineteenth century. Charlotte wrote *Jane Eyre* (1847), Anne wrote *Agnes Grey* (1847), and Emily wrote *Wuthering Heights* (1847).

While *Jane Eyre* drew inspiration from the girls' time at boarding school and *Agnes Grey* was motivated by an impulse toward social reform, Emily took the authoritativeness of the domestic sphere and let it run wild on the page. At once a Gothic tragedy and a twisted love story, *Wuthering Heights* is a novel that simply refuses to be ignored. In the book's characters we observe a Leo's capacity for extremity of emotion—whether through Heathcliff's violent rage and driving passion or Cathy's equally passionate self-focus. Whereas a Pisces-created ghost might briefly materialize (a thing of beauty) and a Gemini ghost might simply forget to show up (ghost party on the moors that night), Cathy's ghost is no shrinking violet. She doesn't float about. No, she bangs on a window, demanding to be heard. "Let me in!" she commands with Leonine authority.

The passion between Cathy and Heathcliff is a lovesick nightmare, to be sure, but it is as much about the self as it is about the other. When Cathy proclaims, "I am Heathcliff," she is fulfilling a classic Leonine dream—to be fully acknowledged and fully seen. To have another soul declare their identity as being fully subsumed by a Leo is about the closest thing to wish fulfillment a Leo is likely to get.

Heathcliff, it's me, I'm Cathy
I've come home, I'm so cold
Let me in your window
—KATE BUSH (LEO),
who shares a birthday with Emily Brontë

As the first and only novel by Emily Brontë, *Wuthering Heights* can give us valuable insight into the author, but she still remains something of a mystery. Much like the sisters' androgynous pseudonyms only drew more attention to and thus speculation about their gender, the fact that Emily published only one book and remains something of a shrouded figure adds to her mystique. One can't help but wonder what her sophomore effort might have looked like. Unfortunately, we'll never know (but see page 51 for one theory). In September 1848, Branwell died, and Emily's health soon deteriorated as well. She died a mere three months later. She was only thirty, and *Wuthering Heights* had been in print only a year. She would never know the success and influence her book would have.

Wuthering Heights is filled with such violent passions, such unresolved ardor, and such mysterious enchantment that it tends to touch a nerve with everyone who reads it, causing some to be repulsed by it and inspiring fanatical devotion in others. It inspired a poem from Sylvia Plath (Scorpio), a vampire series from Stephenie Meyer (Capricorn), and an unforgettable song from fellow Leo Kate Bush. More than a century later, *Wuthering Heights* lives on. Whether you like it or not, it roars.

NOTES FOR WRITERS WITH OTHER LEO PLACEMENTS

WRITER'S CORNER

POSITIVE ASPECTS

You are blessed with veritable buckets of self-confidence. Don't take it for granted.

NEGATIVE ASPECTS

You are a natural leader, but that doesn't mean you always know what you're doing. Seek out valuable guides, mentors, and teachers.

WRITER BEWARE

You can be a little ... haughty. When people help, thank them for it. When people give constructive feedback, consider taking it. If you don't show some humility, others may eventually stop offering support.

LEO MOON: With your dramatic flair and gift for innovation, you are an artistic trailblazer. You are supportive, loyal, and the best cheerleader around. You are an outsized character who lives large and whom many admire. You even have the capacity to be the leader of a new artistic movement.

LEO RISING: A flamboyant leader with a penchant for fun, you are given to extravagant displays, both in your personal life and in your writing. You don't want to write something small that may be forgotten. You have your eye on the Nobel Prize, the canon, and long-lasting fame.

MERCURY IN LEO: Your sentences are apt to be things of utter beauty, your paragraphs organized in such a way that makes them aesthetic masterpieces. When you need to impress, focus on the line, but to push yourself, shift the focus out a little and consider how you might take some of that elegance and expand it to the aesthetics of the overall structure of a piece.

VENUS IN LEO: As a writer, you can cause a scene like no other. You're also apt to write about someone causing a scene with a realism that another sign can only hint at. Take some of that innate drama and magnetic charm and translate it onto the page. You are bound to create some truly memorable characters.

MARS IN LEO: Passionate, driven, and charismatic, you naturally command an audience. The trick for you is to work on trying to be a tad less domineering and on playing a little nicer with others. Accepting some help now and then can never hurt, and it may open up a lot of new avenues for you.

TRY THIS!

+ WRITE a poem about yourself!

+ IMAGINE the most over-the-top, complicated narrative possible. Now write it!

+ WRITE your own autobiography. It doesn't matter if you "haven't done anything yet"—you're a Leo!

READER'S CORNER:
COMPATIBILITY CHART

Which Leo-composed book is most likely to appeal to you? It depends on your sign. Look for your match below. And don't forget to look at your rising and Moon signs, if you know those.

SIGN	CLASSIC	MODERN
ARIES	BEATRIX POTTER, *The Fairy Caravan*	VIKRAM CHANDRA, *Love and Longing in Bombay*
TAURUS	EMILY BRONTË, *Wuthering Heights*	DIANE DI PRIMA, *The Book of Hours*
GEMINI	JOSEPHINE TEY, *The Daughter of Time*	BANANA YOSHIMOTO, *Moshi Moshi*
CANCER	ALDOUS HUXLEY, *Brave New World*	VALERIA LUISELLI, *The Story of My Teeth*
LEO	HERMAN MELVILLE, *Moby-Dick*	ISABEL ALLENDE, *The House of the Spirits*
VIRGO	EDNA FERBER, *Stage Door*	JONATHAN FRANZEN, *The Corrections*

SIGN	CLASSIC	MODERN
LIBRA	GUY DE MAUPASSANT, *Complete Short Stories*	MONA AWAD, *All's Well*
SCORPIO	HELENA BLAVATSKY, *The Secret Doctrine*	CHANG-RAE LEE, *On Such a Full Sea*
SAGITTARIUS	JAMES BALDWIN, *If Beale Street Could Talk*	KRISTEN KITTSCHER, *The Wig in the Window*
CAPRICORN	ALEXANDRE DUMAS, *The Count of Monte Cristo*	ALEX HALEY, *Roots*
AQUARIUS	PERCY BYSSHE SHELLEY, *Prometheus Unbound*	JOHN ASHBERY, *Girls on the Run*
PISCES	CARL JUNG, *Memories, Dreams, Reflections*	LAUREN GROFF, *Arcadia*

VIRGO

VIRGO

THE EXTREME WRITER

BEWARE; FOR I AM FEARLESS,
AND THEREFORE POWERFUL.

—Mary Shelley

VIRGO 101

Virgos have a reputation for being the nitpicking den mothers of the zodiac, but this isn't just unfair, it's an obvious oversimplification. The planet Mercury both rules Virgo and is exalted in Virgo. This means that the Mercurial influence over this sign is stronger than it is in any other placement in the zodiac. Mercury is the planet of communication, and although they may not be as overtly chatty as their Mercurial Gemini sisters, Virgos are absolutely brilliant at communication. They are the editors of the zodiac, gifted with an eye for detail and organizational acumen that would make even a Capricorn jealous.

A mutable earth sign, Virgos are sometimes accused of being unemotional, but this couldn't be further from the truth. They are deeply emotional and filled with love for their families, friends, and neighbors. They simply hold their cards close to their chests. Give a Virgo a chance to open up to you and you will be blessed with the most loyal of friends, but Virgos don't do superficial very well. There is a seriousness to the Virgo heart, and if you think they are unemotional that simply means you haven't created a safe enough space for them to express those emotions.

Virgo rules the 6th House, the house of health and daily work. In modern astrological contexts, this house is often simplified to mean spa visits and board meetings, but in ancient astrology, the 6th House was known as the House of Bad Fortune. We don't tell you this to scare

SIGN OVERVIEW

SYMBOL:
The Maiden

ELEMENT: Earth

QUALITY: Mutable

HOUSE RULED:
6th (Health, Daily Work)

PLANETARY RULER:
Mercury

POSITIVE TRAITS:
Meticulous, Helpful,
Rational

NEGATIVE TRAITS:
Critical, Obsessive,
Judgmental

you, but rather because it is an essential element of the deeper meanings behind the less understood tendencies of this sign. Virgos are concerned with health and well-being—their own, their families', their friends', stray cats'—you get the picture. They will bend over backward to care for a creature in need. While this is indicative of the obvious altruism of the sign, at its core this concern about health is rooted in an anxiety about worst possible outcomes and a desire to be prepared for every eventuality, no matter how grim.

The symbol of Virgo is the maiden of the harvest or, in some traditions, the Greek goddess Persephone herself. It is through Persephone that we come to understand the true nature of the Virgo heart, for while the mind is clear, precise, and detail-oriented, the heart of a Virgo throbs with an undercurrent of anxiety. According to legend, Persephone, the daughter of Demeter, goddess of the harvest, is kidnapped and forced to live in the underworld. Demeter sets about rescuing her daughter but is unable to do so when Persephone breaks a cardinal rule by eating six pomegranate seeds.

Her transgression leaves her trapped in the underworld six months out of the year, one for each seed she consumed. Typically, we regard this myth from Demeter's point of view, using it to explain seasonality and why the world goes dark for half the year when Demeter's grief over her lost daughter cloaks the world in ice, but to understand Virgo, we must imagine Persephone's experience. She is the one who must plunge into that underworld every year. She is the one who must experience this loss of sunlight and earthly bounty. Because of the anticipation of her yearly descent, Persephone must live in a constant state of anxious preparation, knowing that her time of innocence and abundance is limited. What's more, she knows that it is for all of us. We simply don't realize it.

Virgo focuses on what it can control. It sits in the intersection of innocence and experience, of youth and old age, of life and death, and as such, Virgos know that recklessness and impetuous decisions simply aren't a good use of our time. Better to make sure all your ducks are in a row and that your laundry is properly folded and carpet vacuumed, for that matter. This preparation gives them a sense of calm. So, tease them all you want about being obsessive perfectionists who don't know how to cut loose, but know that when the time comes to descend into the underworld, Virgos will be the ones holding the map.

THE VIRGO WRITER:
A LITERARY HISTORY

With their keen understanding of the world's darkness, Virgo writers have put forms to our fears so they may be looked straight in the face. Virgos are analytical and able to respond to collective and personal anxieties of all kinds with a pragmatism so organized it manifests as bravery; they have carried a torch through literary history, lighting the way. Mary Shelley and John William Polidori created monsters that would live in readers' minds for generations, Goethe manipulated the strange mathematics of human relationships, and Tolstoy showed us that an unabashed look at the world's injustices and dangers should lead us to rethink our very outlook on life.

CASE STUDY #1: MARY SHELLEY

Astrologer Chani Nicholas contends that modern assertions that Virgo's symbol is "the virgin" miss the mark. To a twenty-first-century ear, the word *virgin* invokes purity culture and sexual abstinence, but Nicholas argues that, in the realm of Virgo, the idea has more to do with belonging to oneself. For all her involvement with literary historical heavyweights and her intense and life-defining marriage to poet Percy Bysshe Shelley (Leo, see page 106), Virgo genius queen and *Frankenstein* author Mary Shelley truly belonged to herself all her life. Her total defiance of convention left an immortal mark on literary history.

Mary Wollstonecraft Godwin, later Mary Shelley, was born on August 30, 1797. Her mother, Mary Wollstonecraft (Taurus, see page 44), passed away shortly thereafter. Her father was William Godwin (Pisces), a writer and political philosopher who is remembered as an early anarchist and who wrote what is considered by some to be the first mystery (not detective) novel. Godwin's marriage to Wollstonecraft had been very brief and he was left, suddenly, with both little Mary and her half-sister, Fanny Imlay, Wollstonecraft's daughter from a previous relationship.

When Shelley was three, her father remarried, adding two step-siblings to the group. While Shelley's relationship with her stepmother was strained, her stepsister, Clara Mary Jane Clairmont (aka Claire, Taurus), would be an important force and frenemy all her life. In her youth, Shelley spent time in Scotland, and Scotland would play an important role in her fiction. Like her mother, Shelley was intense about her friendships with women, and in Scotland she bonded with her friend Isabel Baxter, returning home once Isabel became engaged to her former brother-in-law, an older man. When Shelley's characters end up in Scotland, you can be sure shit is about to go down.

This brings us to Percy Bysshe Shelley, a radical poet-philosopher and admirer of both Godwin and Wollstonecraft. Percy was drawn to Godwin's home and to Mary, whom he must have seen as a sort of princess of this countercultural intellectual-historical royal family. Mary Shelley started sneaking out to spend time with Percy, who courted her and declared his love on her mother's grave. They also likely consummated their relationship in the churchyard, because, well, Mary was super goth. Godwin tried to separate them but failed—the couple eloped to France in July 1814, leaving behind Percy's pregnant wife and daughter but taking Claire with them.

Why did they do this? Perhaps Mary was influenced by a belief in free love. Possibly she was sick of living with her stepmother. Possibly she was just very infatuated with Percy—and we should remember that when they eloped she was not yet seventeen years old.

We may also look to the influence of Wollstonecraft's ghost. As discussed in her case study, Wollstonecraft was working on a Gothic novel when she died, a bracing critique of social structures that promote inequality. Given the darkness of the text, as well as Wollstonecraft's gruesome death following Mary Shelley's birth, paternal instinct might have led a different father to hide her draft away, or even burn it. But Godwin had published it (though, notably, he destroyed the manuscript), and Shelley, a devoted acolyte of her mother's work, had most likely read it prior to the elopement (indeed, she includes it on her 1814 reading list).

At one point in her unfinished novel, Wollstonecraft's protagonist addresses a daughter who has been torn from her arms. Wollstonecraft writes:

Death may snatch me from you, before you can weigh my advice, or enter into my reasoning: I would then, with fond anxiety, lead you very early in life to form your grand principle of action, to save you from the vain regret of having, through irresolution, let the spring-tide of existence pass away, unimproved, unenjoyed.— Gain experience—ah! gain it—while experience is worth having, and acquire sufficient fortitude to pursue your own happiness; it includes your utility, by a direct path.

By grabbing the hand of a radical thinker and artist, taking her step-sister along for the ride, and heading to France, perhaps the young Mary Shelley may be understood as forming her grand principle of action, as gaining experience while it was worth having. Despite the fact that this choice was motivated, in part, by the writings of both of Mary's parents, Godwin, for his part, was infuriated by the elopement and refused to communicate with Shelley for the next two and a half years.

Mary, Percy, and Claire took a six-week tour through France, Switzerland, Germany, and Holland. The journey was arduous, and shortly after their return to London, Percy went into hiding from his creditors and lived apart from Mary and Claire for a brief period. Always up for a social experiment, Percy encouraged an affair between Mary and his friend Thomas Jefferson Hogg (Gemini); it's possible that Percy was sleeping with Claire at this point and trying to make things "even." For Mary, who was pregnant at the time, the affair was most likely only emotional. She gave birth prematurely and lost the baby, and called on Hogg to comfort her. This immense loss at the age of seventeen would haunt Mary. Following the baby's death, she had a dream of restoring her daughter to life by rubbing her feet by the fire. This dream might have been the first spark of inspiration for *Frankenstein*.

In 1816, Mary gave birth to a son, William, and Claire struck up an affair with renegade celebrity-poet and notorious heartbreaker Lord Byron (Aquarius, see "A Note on Cusp Figures," page 274). When Byron, plagued by scandal that outweighed even his great celebrity, left England, the Shelley party followed him to Switzerland. They rented a house near the shores of Lake Geneva, and Byron inhabited a stately villa nearby. Byron was at this time accompanied by John William Polidori, his personal physician (Virgo, see page 136). The group spent the summer deep in conversation, writing, reading, and exploring the mountains and the lake. Termed "the year without a summer," 1816 saw strange weather patterns and eerie skies, aftershocks of a far-off volcanic eruption. One night, as they were sitting by the fire feeling spooked out by a Coleridge poem, the group decided to write scary stories of their own. And *Frankenstein* came to life.

The drama that marked Mary Shelley's early life only intensified. Of her three children to live past infancy, two died in childhood. In addition

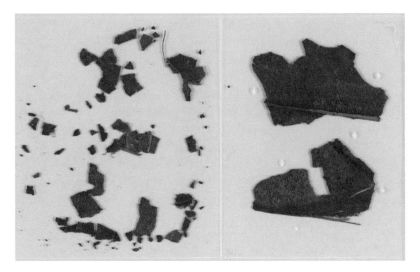

These fragments of Percy Bysshe Shelley's body were treasured by Mary Shelley after his death.

New York Public Library Digital Collections

to these devastating losses, Shelley suffered the loss of her half-sister, Fanny Imlay, who committed suicide. Percy's abandoned wife died of an apparent suicide, and while he would never regain custody of his children, this did allow Percy and Mary to marry. Mary Shelley reconciled with her father, but their relationship remained complicated, and he confiscated Shelley's little-known novella *Mathilda*. The Shelleys' marriage was happy and collaborative but also intense and marked by his unfaithfulness and general bad behavior. And then suddenly Percy was gone, drowned while sailing. He was cremated, and Shelley treasured fragments of his body all her life, because, again, super goth. Percy's death occurred only a couple of weeks after Shelley suffered a miscarriage so bloody, it almost killed her.

We tend to remember Shelley as a brilliant young ingenue, but she was also a Virgo bar none. From Percy's death in 1822 until her own in 1851, Shelley was a badass working writer and single mom. She moved from genre to genre, producing airtight doorstoppers and working her fingers to the bone to care for and maintain custody of her surviving son, a delicate dance that involved her aristocratic, disapproving father-in-law. An ally to friends whose sexual and gender identities were marginalized and in some cases persecuted in England, Shelley at one point helped Walter Sholto Douglas (who would most likely have identified as a trans man today) and Isabella Robinson obtain false passports and travel to Paris as husband and wife. As she neared the end of her life, Shelley made sure her son was well married to a wealthy young widow who would both adore

Virgos often have a talent for meticulous record-keeping. If that sounds like you, we recommend channeling this talent to your advantage. Cultivating a daily practice of listing your favorite moments, meals, and conversations can help you find cognitive balance so you don't get too bogged down by the world's woes.

him and work to preserve the Shelley family's literary legacy. No matter what they've been through, Virgos manage to get the job done.

CASE STUDY #2: JOHN WILLIAM POLIDORI

Dubbed "Polly Dolly" and "Poor Polidori" by his circumstantial literary circle, John William Polidori was that rare literary figure who makes a genre-defining mark on literary history while remaining a total flop. Born on September 7, 1795, the child of a Tuscan scholar/translator father and an English mother, Polidori would be connected to literary giants all his life, yet never truly shine on his own. (Notably, his sister, Frances, would one day count among her children Victorian poets Dante Gabriel [Taurus] and Christina Rossetti [Sagittarius].) While among Byron and the Shelleys in 1816, Polidori wrote that he felt "like a star in the halo of the moon, invisible." The writers around Polidori told him his literary productions were worth nothing. Luckily for literary history, Polidori would channel his pettiness and hurt feelings into the creation of a monster that would shape vampire literature for decades to come.

Polidori received his doctorate in medicine at the remarkable age of nineteen. His thesis, which focused on somnambulism, would have a tremendous influence on his vampire story and on vampire stories to come. While he seemed on track for a productive career in medicine, Polidori confided in his diary that he was "ambitious for literary distinction" and was happy to accept Lord Byron's invitation to go on a trip to the continent as his personal physician. Byron's publisher offered Polidori five hundred pounds to keep a journal of the trip, a record that, if preserved in its entirety, might offer us rare and scintillating clues about Byron and the Shelleys. Unfortunately for gossips of the future, however, Polidori's aunt got to it first and removed the passages she found distasteful.

Anecdotes about Polidori's time on the shores of Lake Geneva give us a good sense of his try-hard nature and social and literary frustrations.

He seems to have had a crush on Mary Shelley, and hurt his ankle in an attempt to jump off a wall to impress her. While most scholars have skirted the possibility that Byron and Polidori were involved romantically, we think Polidori probably at least had a crush on Byron, too. As friends and traveling colleagues of sorts, Byron and Polidori didn't really get along and tended to bicker about stupid stuff.

Alas, we don't have Polidori's unedited journal from this period. What we do have, however, is *The Vampyre.* Remember that dark and stormy night when a ghost story contest inspired Mary Shelley to begin working in earnest on *Frankenstein?* In response to that contest, Byron produced only a fragment. This fragment, however, does contain a haunting image in which a slain man begs his traveling companion not to reveal the secret of his demise. In response to this

YOU MIGHT BE A VIRGO IF:
you're not petty. You're really not, okay? You're just inspired by people, and people sometimes suck.

scene, Polidori wrote *The Vampyre*—a reinvention of the classic monster that totally drags Byron. Like Byron, Polidori's Vampyre is a seductive, debauched aristocrat. Like Byron, he devours women and destroys men. When the Vampyre puts his male traveling companion under an oath of secrecy, one that his companion cannot break no matter whom his secret puts in danger, it's hard not to wonder whether some unspoken bond pulsed beneath the surface of Byron and Polidori's tense relationship.

Byron dismissed Polidori only five months later. Polidori continued his tour of Switzerland on foot, wound up at the theater with Byron and a friend, who were passing through, complained too obnoxiously about an Austrian grenadier's hat that was obstructing his view of the stage, and got kicked out of town. He treated some members of the English colony in Pisa, all of whom died under his care, and then set up a medical practice in Norwich. His fiction, other than *The Vampyre*, was largely ignored; his poetry was praised and then forgotten.

Simply put, Polidori never broke through as a writer on his own terms. You see, *The Vampyre* probably only ever appeared in print because it was sent along by an acquaintance. It was at first attributed to Byron, which fanned the flames of its popularity and led to stage adaptations, but when Byron claimed his name was used in vain, Polidori came off as a plagiarist and an operator. Polidori's literary dreams were crushed, and the writers he knew felt a bit like bullies. He suffered a bad concussion, abandoned medicine, enrolled in law school, and, most likely, took his own life. But while Polidori didn't live the life or achieve the success he wanted, his annoyance or frustration or desire or *whatever* with Lord Byron shifted the way we in the Anglo-American tradition would think about vampires forever. Whenever you see a rich, sexy vampire engaging in the art of seduction, remember that on some level you're really looking at Byron. So if Edward in *Twilight* is really Byron, and *Fifty Shades of Grey* is *Twilight* fan fiction, then *Fifty Shades of Grey* is about having sex with Byron.

READING LIST:

Sexy Vampires

1. THE VAMPYRE by John William Polidori (Virgo)

2. CARMILLA by J. Sheridan Le Fanu (Virgo)

3. INTERVIEW WITH THE VAMPIRE by Anne Rice (Libra)

4. DEAD UNTIL DARK by Charlaine Harris (Sagittarius)

CASE STUDY #3: JOHANN WOLFGANG VON GOETHE

Known to posterity as the greatest German writer of all time, Johann Wolfgang von Goethe was a literary movement all his own. Celebrated for his poetry, fiction, and drama, and also for his scientific forays into geology, botany, anatomy, physics, and so on, he was the ultimate Virgo person of inquiry: a moment in one man. What in British literary history is often called the Romantic period was, in Germany, sometimes known simply as the Age of Goethe.

Raised by stately, educated parents dedicated to his erudition, Goethe studied art, music, and languages from a young age, sometimes shaping his school exercises into the form of novels. A combination of factors including fairs, trade, and the presence of French soldiers during the Seven Years' War gave Goethe's childhood home of Frankfurt a bustling, connected, cosmopolitan feel. While they can be emotionally rigid, Virgos often crave a sense of intellectual expansion; the combination of city life and his thoughtful course of study offered this opportunity to young Goethe.

While Goethe pursued a variety of fields, he was a prolific writer from a young age. In 1779, his sentimental epistolary novel, *The Sorrows of Young Werther*, became a breakout success. The heartrending story of a scorned lover who takes his own life capitalized on current trends and took them to the level of storytelling perfection. In the novel, a sensitive, sentimental artist who might have been called *emo* in the early aughts experiences a rejection from a woman who is already engaged. Werther spends time with both the woman and her betrothed, putting himself through emotional torture and openly acknowledging that one member of the love triangle must die in order to resolve the situation. With unbending emotional affect and an unbreakable adherence to form, Werther backs himself into a corner from which suicide is the only escape.

In writing *Werther*, Goethe was in part sending up the sentimentalism of the age, because of course one doesn't have to die just because one's crush is already committed to somebody else, and the mathematical proof Werther applies to prove that his own time is up is not sound. Frustratingly for Goethe, however, readers didn't understand that the book was a cultural critique. As he invented the Age of Goethe, Goethe also criticized the very sentimentality that he peddled. This kind of unapologetic doubling—of strategy and the truth—can define a Virgo writer on the rise.

And Goethe was certainly on the rise. For the last thirty years of his life he was Germany's greatest cultural monument, and folks traveled from all over the world to pay their respects, first to the man himself and then to the town of Weimar, in which he had lived.

Goethe's 1809 novel, *Elective Affinities*, is his most Virgo work of prose. While ostensibly a sentimental love story of sorts, the novel is really a dark mathematical playbook. Two childhood friends, Eduard and Charlotte, having lost their first spouses, marry each other and generally enjoy life on a secluded, aristocratic estate. But their perfect equilibrium is upset by two outsiders: Captain Otto, a friend of Eduard's, and Ottilie, Charlotte's niece. These guests are appealing in various ways, and the pairings begin to mix and remix, the social experiment becoming almost palpable as a scientific experiment. In fact, the characters discuss this way of looking at things:

Sometimes [things] will meet as friends and old acquaintances who hasten together and unite without changing one another in any way, as wine mixes with water. On the other hand, there are others who will remain obdurate strangers to one another and refuse to unite in any way even through mechanical mixing and grinding, as oil and water shaken together will a moment later separate again.

As they mix and remix with ultimately disastrous consequences, the characters at the novel's heart understand how this strange system of combinatorics applies to themselves. And herein lies a poignant warning to any Virgo writer, or perhaps any Virgo in general. Rules exist for a reason, but if you adhere to them too strictly, someone might get hurt because people are people, not numbers or coins or chemical substances. When people are involved, systems and structures can only get you so far.

CODA: LEO TOLSTOY

Count Lev Nikolayevich Tolstoy, better known in English as Leo Tolstoy, born on September 9, 1828, to an aristocratic Russian family, is widely regarded as one of the greatest writers of all time. While he was first recognized for the semiautobiographical writings of his twenties, which focused on youth and drew from his experiences in the Crimean War, he is best known today for the novels *War and Peace* (1869) and *Anna Karenina* (1878). These world-historical classics are held up as landmark examples of the realist novel, meaning they adhere to the depth and complexity of reality and pay close attention to the systems and structures that define people's lives in the real world. It may come as no surprise that these famous, immortal realist novels came from the pen of a Virgo writer, as Virgos are blessed with sharp, analytical minds and are often able to see the world from various and sometimes even opposing perspectives.

READING LIST:
Great Realist Novels

1. MANSFIELD PARK by Jane Austen (Sagittarius)

2. MIDDLEMARCH by George Eliot (Sagittarius)

3. MADAME BOVARY by Gustave Flaubert (Sagittarius)

4. BLEAK HOUSE by Charles Dickens (Aquarius)

5. ANNA KARENINA and WAR AND PEACE by Leo Tolstoy (Virgo)

In addition to his most famous novels, Tolstoy wrote across genres. His corpus includes short stories, novellas, and plays, as well as philosophical, socioeconomic, and theological works. Virgos' ability to take a clear and uncompromising look at the world around them can sometimes stoke pragmatic activist tendencies, and by the 1870s Tolstoy was undergoing a philosophical transformation, revising his moral code to define himself as a Christian anarchist and pacifist. This change caused some marital drama for him, but once a Virgo has made up their mind about an ethical commitment, it's difficult to shake their resolve regardless of the consequences. Tolstoy would preach nonviolent resistance for the rest of his life, and his ideas would influence important figures including Mahatma Gandhi (Aquarius) and Martin Luther King Jr. (Capricorn). Unlike, say, Polidori, who took the world's cruelty personally and simply couldn't bear it, the example of Tolstoy reveals the Virgo's unique ability to see the world as it is and to make and keep commitments accordingly.

NOTES FOR WRITERS WITH OTHER VIRGO PLACEMENTS

WRITER'S CORNER

POSITIVE ASPECTS

With your gift for communication and perfectionistic linguistic flair, you can make any sentence shine.

NEGATIVE ASPECTS

You may need to be strict about negative self-talk while drafting. There will be plenty of time for your legendarily critical eye to have at the manuscript once it's finished.

WRITER BEWARE

You may have a tendency toward a kind of hypochondria with your writing. Not everything needs to be fixed. Some things aren't broken.

VIRGO MOON: You are highly empathetic and most likely take care of everyone around you, especially when it comes to health. However, your emotions tend to be caught up in the details of daily life and you may be beset by worries. Focus on positive possibilities to work toward overcoming some of your anxiety. Because you are a quick study of all things health-related, wellness writing may be an area in which you thrive.

VIRGO RISING: You have a nearly unmatched flair for detail and are quite gifted at math, science, and anything analytical. Writing that involves a lot of research may be a draw for you. You ooze efficiency and give the general impression that you know exactly what you're doing even when you don't. As such, you would cut a formidable editorial figure and would do well to be at the helm of a publishing venture.

MERCURY IN VIRGO: Mercury in Virgo endows you with an excellent mind for facts and figures as well as the ability to maintain multiple projects at once. You may work in more than one genre. Make sure not to overload yourself with too many ventures and risk losing track of them all. Limit yourself to a few key passion projects and you should be good to go.

VENUS IN VIRGO: Venus in Virgo can give you a keen editorial eye for finding faults—perhaps too keen an eye. Although your ability to find a split infinitive in a haystack is admirable, if you focus too much on flaws you risk losing sight of the big picture. Make sure to spend some time thinking about what is working in your writing before you tear it all to pieces.

MARS IN VIRGO: You can keep track of every aspect of a manuscript (or even several manuscripts) without so much as batting an eye. You are a veritable spreadsheet of a person, capable of creating intensely complicated literary works. Does the mystery genre appeal to you? You will deal out those clues with the skill of a master croupier. Is science writing more your thing? You basically are a living, breathing taxonomy. Whatever kind of writing interests you, you bring to it a brilliant attention to detail and a drive toward absolute perfection.

TRY THIS!

+ **THINK** of a person who rubs you the wrong way. Then write a monster narrative based on that person's behaviors.

+ **EXPERIMENT** with ethnographic writing. You might spend time in an unfamiliar place writing down everything you notice, interview an acquaintance about what makes them tick, or try a written sketch of the various forces and historical events that have shaped your own life and identity.

+ **TRY** activist writing—it may appeal to you. Start small with an op-ed on a local topic that gets you fired up.

READER'S CORNER:
COMPATIBILITY CHART

Which Virgo-composed book is most likely to appeal to you? It depends on your sign. Look for your match below. And don't forget to look at your rising and Moon signs if you know those.

SIGN	CLASSIC	MODERN
ARIES	O. HENRY, *Selected Short Stories*	JENNIFER EGAN, *A Visit from the Goon Squad*
TAURUS	D. H. LAWRENCE, *Sons and Lovers*	SONIA SANCHEZ, *Shake Loose My Skin*
GEMINI	DANIEL DEFOE, *Robinson Crusoe*	ALEXANDER CHEE, *How to Write an Autobiographical Novel*
CANCER	WILLIAM CARLOS WILLIAMS, *Spring and All*	ALISON BECHDEL, *Fun Home: A Family Tragicomic*
LEO	AGATHA CHRISTIE, *Murder on the Orient Express*	LEONARD COHEN, *The Flame*
VIRGO	MARY SHELLEY, *The Last Man*	HANYA YANAGIHARA, *A Little Life*

SIGN	CLASSIC	MODERN
LIBRA	H.D., *Collected Poems*	TONY TULATHIMUTTE, *Private Citizens*
SCORPIO	LEO TOLSTOY, *Anna Karenina*	STEPHEN KING, *The Shining*
SAGITTARIUS	JOHN WILLIAM POLIDORI, *Ernestus Berchtold; or, The Modern Oedipus: A Tale*	SAMANTHA HUNT, *The Unwritten Book: An Investigation*
CAPRICORN	JOHANN WOLFGANG VON GOETHE, *Faust*	RITA DOVE, *Collected Poems 1974–2004*
AQUARIUS	JEAN RHYS, *Wide Sargasso Sea*	JOE SACKSTEDER, *Make/Shift*
PISCES	JORGE LUIS BORGES, *Labyrinths*	JULIO CORTÁZAR, *Hopscotch*

LIBRA

THE WRITER ON THE BRINK

I CAN RESIST EVERYTHING
EXCEPT TEMPTATION.

—Oscar Wilde

LIBRA 101

More than any other sign in the zodiac, Libra is known for its relationship to balance. An air sign ruled by Venus, Libra rules the 7th House of partnership. As such, Librans have the uncanny ability to take two fundamentally different—even opposing—elements and synthesize them to create a balanced whole. Libras are often accused of being indecisive, forever vacillating between poles of possibility rather than setting down a stake and claiming a solid position. Although this indecisiveness can rear its head now and again—woe be it to anyone who tries to rush a Libra while they're deciding on a sartorial decision—this is a misapprehension of Libra's gift. Their ability to see multiple sides of a situation means that they are able to understand the very nature of opposition, and that's an extraordinary thing.

Libras make phenomenal mediators and diplomats. They excel at all kinds of negotiation. In fact, negotiation is their default setting. Rare is the Libra who can turn a blind eye to injustice, but rarer still is the Libra who rushes into direct confrontation with it. Their legendary vacillation actually speaks of a compulsion toward peace. While their opposite sign, Aries, might rush in precipitously and cause explosive conflict where none need exist, Libra will ruminate and reflect. They will be absolutely certain before they confront, and when they do, it will be with their intoxicating personal magnetism and silver-tongued wit.

SIGN OVERVIEW

SYMBOL:
The Scales

ELEMENT: Air

QUALITY: Cardinal

HOUSE RULED:
7th (Partnership)

PLANETARY RULER:
Venus

POSITIVE TRAITS:
Balanced, Diplomatic,
Charming

NEGATIVE TRAITS:
Indecisive, Acquisitive,
Beauty-Obsessed

These Venusian charmers are consummate aesthetes. They have an innate eye for design and a natural sense of style. They like their environments to be elegantly appointed, even luxe, and you will often find them dressed to the nines in fashion that is both divinely appealing and sensuous to wear. Like their fellow air sign Gemini, Libras are chatters. They thrive on human interaction. A deeply humanitarian impulse runs through the Libran heart, but unlike their Aquarian air siblings, Libras' propensity toward humanitarianism is a product of their deep love of giving. Idealistic almost to a fault, Libras can sometimes become impractical in their quest for peaceful equilibrium. Much to their chagrin, not everything can be easily unified, and not everyone shares their altruistic goals of worldwide harmony, equality, and justice.

Although Libras embody the playful contradiction of their fellow air sign Gemini, as well as the aesthetic brilliance of their Venus-ruled cousin, Taurus, there is a gravitas to the sign that is often overlooked. Not only is Libra the beginning of the transition to the winter months (and the sign can inhabit some of the colder qualities of the season), it is also the sign in which Saturn is exalted, or especially powerful. Because Saturn is the planet associated with misfortune, there can be a bit of a heaviness to Libra. There is even a tendency in some cases for a Libra's quest for beauty to turn to hedonism, for their idealism to become overly judgmental, and for their love of contradiction to become an exploration of the more haunting aspects of the human psyche.

Above all, though, *love* is the catchword for Libra. They love to love and they can find a reason to love almost anyone and anything. Their ability to hold multiple contrasting variables in their head at one time means that they can see the ugliness in you so clearly that to them it becomes beauty. Libras were born wearing rose-colored glasses.

THE LIBRA WRITER:
A LITERARY HISTORY

Libra writers often combine a flamboyant style and love of aesthetics with a humanitarian drive and an interest in tragic beauty. Horace Walpole lived for human connection but wrote about gloomy, haunted castles. Frances Ellen Watkins Harper fought fiercely for equality while also being prodigiously gifted as an artist. Oscar Wilde strove to create art for art's sake, and Samuel Taylor Coleridge attempted to integrate his yearning for love with his impulse to self-destruct. Libra writers fight for causes, challenge our senses, and live at the cutting edge of both society and art.

CASE STUDY #1: HORACE WALPOLE

In a sign known for its captivating extravagance and ability to synthesize contradiction, we find the man who not only invented an entire genre of contradictory impulses, but did so while living in an outlandish Gothic revival castle that he fancifully named Strawberry Hill.

Even by birth, Walpole was thoroughly Libran. Born into the lap of luxury, he was the youngest son of beautiful socialite Catherine Shorter and Britain's first prime minister, Sir Robert Walpole (Virgo). Whether Horace was in fact his father's son, though, is a matter of some controversy. By the time of his birth, more than a decade after that of his nearest sibling, the Walpoles were basically estranged. In appearance, Horace took solely after his mother. Was he a rightful descendant of the crème de la crème of British aristocracy, or was he the outcome of his mother's passionate dalliance? It is thoroughly Libra to occupy both spaces at once.

Walpole coined the term "serendipity."

Sometimes Libras can be accused of being so equivocating that they become lazy with indecision. This is often the furthest thing from the truth (see Frances Ellen Watkins Harper, Libra, page 156), but in Walpole's case there may be some truth in the critique, at least in his youth. Walpole attended the best schools (Eton, followed by Cambridge), but he failed to earn a degree. He served in Parliament as a Whig politician but was not terrifically involved in the undertaking. What he did excel at were the typical Libran traits of diplomacy, social acumen, and general conviviality. Friendship was deeply important to Walpole. He was a wildly popular man who walked ceaselessly to the beat of his own drum. Clad in lavender velvet suits and deeply sensitive, he made many friends, especially among women. Various biographers have posited that he might have been gay, but if we take Walpole at face value and give credence to this intentional celibacy, we discover a space of pure Libran expression. He seems to have identified as asexual, and most likely never took a romantic partner. Libras love their fellow humans with unparalleled ardor, but that love doesn't have to be sexual in nature. Because Libra is ruled by Venus, the planet concerned with beauty and love in all its forms, in many ways the apotheosis of Libra is to love through friendship.

Libras are particular about their environment, and Walpole was no exception. In 1747, Walpole started construction on a Gothic Revival castle he called Strawberry Hill. He transformed a cottage into a magnificent Gothic castle, with historically accurate architectural features like battlements and looming towers, and forty-six acres of breathtaking gardens. Although the monstrosity

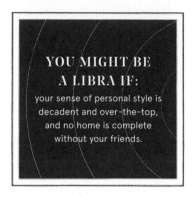

YOU MIGHT BE A LIBRA IF:

your sense of personal style is decadent and over-the-top, and no home is complete without your friends.

speaks of Libra's desire for excess in all things beautiful, it also speaks of a Libra's penchant for thumbing its nose at conventional mores. As biographer Timothy Mowl writes, "His taste as expressed in Strawberry Hill was one of deliberate rebel counter-culture." At Strawberry Hill, Walpole was almost constantly surrounded by friends, and he even brought his closest companions, the Berry sisters, to come and live with him. Walpole often referred to Agnes (Gemini) and Mary (Pisces) Berry as his "twin wives," though their relationship was almost undoubtedly platonic, especially since Mary was likely gay herself. The three of them threw lavish parties and created something of an artistic oasis, sought out by like-minded aesthetes.

Walpole established a printing press at Strawberry Hill—one of the first. Like most Libras, Walpole was deeply upset by inhumanity, violence, and injustice of any kind. An abolitionist and liberal, he used the press to compose political pamphlets with humanitarian vigor. Walpole was deeply concerned with the suffering of his fellow man. "The world is a comedy to those that think, a tragedy to those that feel," he once wrote to a friend.

In addition to political writing and art history essays, Walpole published three novels, the first of which, *The Castle of Otranto* (1764), is often considered the first Gothic novel. Written seemingly for amusement and self-published at Strawberry Hill, *Otranto* is a sensationalistic novel about familial curses, incest, and revenge. Purported to be a found text of unknown authorship and translated from its original Italian, *Otranto* is an over-the-top extravaganza of fanciful prose. As such, it has Libra written all over it. Walpole eventually claimed authorship. It's something of a convoluted story about a man who, in trying to avoid a prophecy, sets off a series of misunderstandings and misadventures, complete with murdered brides, ghosts, and comically gigantic suits of armor.

In *The Castle of Otranto,* Walpole sought to marry the sentimental with the horrible, and thus created the Gothic novel with all its dark hallways, imperiled heroines, and tainted bloodlines. Integrating these contradictory aesthetics created a pleasant kind of terror, a hallmark of the genre. (For more about the Gothic, see Ann Radcliffe, page 90, and Matthew "Monk" Lewis, page 93—both Cancers.)

A portrait of Horace Walpole, Earl of Orford; Strawberry Hill.

New York Public Library
Digital Collections

The Castle of Otranto received mixed reviews, but it would set a course for the Gothic genre that we are still happily traveling today. After *Otranto,* Walpole published two more books, *The Mysterious Mother: A Tragedy* (1768), a controversial novel that dealt once again with incest, and *Hieroglyphic Tales* (1785), a collection of short stories. In his final years, Walpole returned to writing about political concerns before dying in 1797 at the ripe old age of eighty.

CASE STUDY #2: FRANCES ELLEN WATKINS HARPER

If Walpole expressed his Libran love of humanity through his friendships, Frances Ellen Watkins Harper did so on a much more epic scale. An important writer and activist during her time, Harper was once a household name but has since all but disappeared from the public consciousness. Born to free parents in Maryland, Johnson was tragically orphaned at the age of three. After her parents'

YOU MIGHT BE A LIBRA IF:
you consume media voraciously and love all genres equally.

deaths, she was raised by her aunt and uncle, whose guidance would help her find her mission in life. Her uncle was a scholar and abolitionist who, in addition to practicing medicine, ran a school that Harper attended until age thirteen. After leaving school, Harper went to work as a domestic servant for a family of Quakers who ran a bookshop. Because she was given free access to the breadth of the shop's offerings, it was in her employers' bookshop that Harper satisfied her voracious appetite for the written word. Every writer is a reader first, and that early access to literature most likely inspired Harper to develop her gifts. Her innate agility with language, her depth of knowledge, and her deep concern for the human condition would ultimately align to cement her signature style.

Harper began writing early and proved something of a prodigy as a poet, publishing her first volume (*Forest Leaves*, 1846) at the age of twenty-one. At twenty-six, Harper left her home state of Maryland to take a job as the first female instructor at Union Seminary in Columbus, Ohio. Teaching suited Harper well, but as gifted as she was as a writer and a teacher, she was destined for even greater things. She moved in with prominent abolitionist friends of her uncle, William (Libra) and Letitia George Still, and under their tutelage became a deeply influential activist and speaker. Horrified by injustice in all its forms, she devoted herself to advocating for equality. She was active in the Underground Railroad and became well known on the abolitionist circuit.

In 1860, she married Fenton Harper, who had three children of his own and with whom she had a daughter, Mary. Fenton died only four years after they wed. Because women couldn't own property and because her husband died in debt, creditors took everything from Harper, leaving her homeless and with no way to feed her four charges.

Undeterred, Harper made a living as a writer and speaker, becoming one of the most influential activists of her time and the first African American woman to publish a short story. She also wrote several novels and became the most popular African American poet of her time. Harper was able to become both a successful activist and an established artist, which speaks to Libra's abilities not only to exist in multiple realms and divergent spaces, but to dominate them.

In addition to being almost preternaturally able to overcome adversity and loss, Harper inspired countless others and served as a fierce advocate for those less fortunate. In addition to working with Frederick Douglass to form the American Woman Suffrage Association, she was the cofounder and vice president of the National Association of Colored Women's Clubs, the superintendent of the Colored Sections of the Philadelphia and Pennsylvania Women's Christian Temperance Unions, and the director of the American Association of Colored Youth.

Harper's written work tackled themes of justice, dealing unflinchingly with social issues, racism, feminism, and classism. Her poetry is infused with a potent combination of Libra beauty and boldness, with an eye toward the natural world. Take, for example, her short poem "I Thirst" (see page 158):

FIRST VOICE

I thirst, but earth cannot allay
The fever coursing through my veins,
The healing stream is far away—
It flows through Salem's lovely plains.

The murmurs of its crystal flow
Break ever o'er this world of strife;
My heart is weary, let me go,
To bathe it in the stream of life;

For many worn and weary hearts
Have bathed in this pure healing stream,
And felt their griefs and cares depart,
E'en like some sad forgotten dream.

SECOND VOICE

"The Word is nigh thee, even in thy heart."

Say not, within thy weary heart,
Who shall ascend above,
To bring unto thy fever'd lips
The fount of joy and love.

Nor do thou seek to vainly delve
Where death's pale angels tread,
To hear the murmur of its flow
Around the silent dead.

Within, in thee is one living fount,
Fed from the springs above;
There quench thy thirst till thou shalt bathe
In God's own sea of love.

Harper draws on the beauty of nature and the promise of spirituality, all while locating the ability to attain those precious gifts within the self.

Her short story "The Two Offers" is an overtly feminist work about two women born into different means whose life paths diverge based on their choice of a marital partner. One woman, who is well off, contemplates two offers of marriage, ultimately deciding on the more romantically inclined of the suitors. Her cousin, who comes from a more modest background, counsels the first woman to hold off on making her choice. She advises that an unhappy marriage can be disastrous for a woman, and an institution in which she is essentially treated as property is a dangerous thing to enter without great consideration. The first woman ends up marrying an abusive philanderer whose wicked ways ultimately lead to her death. The cousin, more concerned about her autonomy, decides to delay marriage until late in life, by which time she has become a successful and happy woman in her own right. "Two Offers," written in the sentimental style so popular at that time, is essentially a morality story concerned with feminist ideals, but it is also a Libra tale through and through. The story speaks of freedom, justice, even beauty, and is as much a tale of love and idealism as it is a cry against injustice.

But while Harper shone as a poet and a fiction writer, it was her rhetorical gifts that truly set her apart. In her most famous speech, "We Are All Bound Up Together," Harper evinces Libran idealism while also holding disparate realities within a single space. She speaks of how all humankind is bound up together and that by hurting one another we only hurt ourselves. She shows how racism and slavery are immoral and have had negative effects on every segment of society, save for those directly profiting from the atrocity. She also speaks unflinchingly about class, saying:

> This grand and glorious revolution which has commenced, will fail to reach its climax of success, until throughout the length and breadth of the American Republic, the nation shall be so

color-blind, as to know no man by the color of his skin or the curl of his hair. It will then have no privileged class, trampling upon and outraging the unprivileged classes, but will be then one great privileged nation, whose privilege will be to produce the loftiest manhood and womanhood that humanity can attain.

Harper goes on to caution her audience that giving women the right to vote will not necessarily serve as a panacea to the racism and bigotry that afflict the country. She points out that not all white women will be abolitionists. She intimates that it is naïve to think so. Instead, she says, she fears that white women will divide into similar factions as white men: the good, the bad, and the indifferent. "The good would vote according to their convictions and principles," she says, "the bad as dictated by prejudice or malice; and the indifferent will vote in the strongest side of the question, with the winning party."

Libras, more than any other sign, understand that
the cup is both half full and half empty.

In that speech, given at the eleventh National Women's Rights Convention in 1866, Harper spoke about what would come to be called *intersectionality*, essentially positing that as an African American woman, she faced different struggles than did her white colleagues and that to ignore this fact could be disastrous.

The fact that Harper has fallen so far out of the popular consciousness is a great loss. A brilliant writer, orator, and dedicated activist, she embodied the most high-minded aspects of her sign: altruism, humanitarianism, and diplomacy. She was able to use the beauty of language to affect the way people thought, fought, and voted. She died of heart failure at the age of eighty-five, nine years before women would earn the right to vote.

CASE STUDY #3: OSCAR WILDE

Oscar Wilde, circa 1882.
He could, as the kids say, get it.

New York Public Library Digital Collections

It's not a coincidence that one of the greatest, most-quoted wits of all time was born under the sign of Libra. The middle child of a successful poet, Jane (Capricorn), and a prominent surgeon and writer, William, Oscar Wilde was born in Dublin in 1854. Schooled at home until the age of nine, Wilde showed a gift for languages. He attended Trinity College where he lived with his brother Willie (Virgo) and excelled academically, earning a scholarship to continue his studies at Oxford. At Oxford, while still maintaining a reputation as a "bad boy" (Libras love to play the rebel), Wilde continued to thrive, making a name for himself as much for his intellect as for his flamboyant style and fancy dress. No one has ever accused Libras of being a bunch of shrinking violets.

Because they are ruled by Venus, Libras are often said to possess an inherent beauty they might have lacked had they been born under a different sign. There is no doubt that Wilde both appreciated beauty and created a sense of decadent visual sensualism wherever he went. This wasn't always appreciated, but it drew attention and informed his view of art, which he felt was "inherently useless," but nonetheless important. He didn't believe that art must have a moral or political valence to be important, but rather should be created because it had value in its own right. This rebellious attitude, rooted in the Decadent movement of the late nineteenth century, stood in stark contrast to the predominating Victorian values that held that art should primarily be didactic and serve moral and sociopolitical ends. "The artist should never try to be popular," Wilde maintained. "Rather, the public should be more artistic."

At twenty-one, Wilde became transfixed by notorious beauty Florence Balcombe (Cancer), and the two dated for some time before growing apart. She went on to marry none other than Bram Stoker (Scorpio, page 179). Eventually Wilde settled down with Constance Lloyd (Capricorn), with whom he had two children and a fairly congenial marriage. When Wilde became romantically involved with a series of younger men, Constance seemed to have taken it in stride. By all accounts, she had a taste for freedom herself and could not be contained placidly within the confines of marriage. As such, Wilde seems to have lived for a while as a fairly open homosexual during a time when it was not just unusual to do so—it was illegal.

Wilde lived ecstatically and with a great sense of humor about himself, and his writing evinces a similar levity and elegant wit. He's the man who gave us such quips as "The public is wonderfully tolerant. It forgives everything except genius" and "I don't want to go to Heaven. None of my friends are there," as well as "Experience is the name men give to their mistakes." He gave us the height of farce in the brilliant *The Importance of Being Earnest* (1895) as well as the wonderful absurdity of *Lady Windermere's Fan* (1892).

While Wilde was inarguably a comic genius, there is also an undercurrent of sadness that floats just beneath the surface of his work, at times surging forth with great power. If Gothic sentiment is on full display in Walpole's work, it infuses Wilde's work with a depth that belies the sign's more obvious ebullience. Although Wilde's childhood was, for the most part, a happy one, it was marked by a tragedy that weighed deeply on him throughout his days. When he was only twelve, his dearly beloved younger sister, Isola (Aries), died suddenly. He was devastated by her death, and as a boy he visited her grave often. His heartache over the loss is on full display in his poem "Requiescat" (1881).

Tread lightly, she is near
    Under the snow,
Speak gently, she can hear
    The daisies grow.
All her bright golden hair
    Tarnished with rust,
She that was young and fair
    Fallen to dust.
Lily-like, white as snow,
    She hardly knew
She was a woman, so
    Sweetly she grew.
Coffin-board, heavy stone,
    Lie on her breast,
I vex my heart alone
    She is at rest.
Peace, Peace, she cannot hear
    Lyre or sonnet,
All my life's buried here,
    Heap earth upon it.

These are not the words of an ambivalent, indecisive air sign. There is a depth here that speaks to Libra's less obvious qualities. Similarly, his most popular novel, *The Picture of Dorian Gray* (1890), is a masterwork in combining the luxe and the Gothic. A *Faust* retelling, the novel concerns a young man so consumed with youth and beauty that he sells his soul to maintain it. The book deals directly with the more tenebrous side of Libran impulses—vanity, hedonism, the drive to excess—but it also touches on injustice, highlighting just how much damage Dorian's solipsism did to those around him.

In the popular imagination, Wilde is forever imbued with a potent wit and acerbic hilarity, but in actuality, he died a broken, destitute man, a victim of a society that criminalized homosexuality. Wilde had been at the top of his game, having recently written *The Importance of Being Earnest* and *The Picture of Dorian Gray*, as well as *An Ideal Husband* (1893). But he was to become the victim of a vicious legal assault carried out by the father of one of his romantic partners. As a result, Wilde was imprisoned for two years. When he was released, he was destitute and in ill health. He managed to write *The Ballad of Reading Gaol* (1898), a serious poem that outlined the inhumanity of the prison system, before dying in 1900 of meningitis. It is truly heartbreaking that a writer who gave so much could have his life stolen by the evils of bigotry and hate.

CODA: SAMUEL TAYLOR COLERIDGE

As we near the cusp of Libra and edge into Scorpio, we see more of that wintry chill in the inscrutable figure of Samuel Taylor Coleridge. Born in Ottery St. Mary in 1772, Coleridge was the youngest son of a vicar and schoolmaster. A shy boy, he was a voracious reader, eventually studying at Cambridge where he excelled academically, but failed to graduate, instead enlisting anonymously in the dragoons at the age of twenty-one.

It was on a walking tour of Oxford that he met poet Robert Southey (Leo). The two became fast friends and were inspired to collaborate in the creation of what they termed a "pantisocracy" in which they envisioned a communal egalitarian utopia inspired by Plato's *Republic*. However, their proposed utopia didn't come to fruition.

Coleridge married Southey's sister-in-law and childhood friend Sara (née Fricker), but the marriage would prove a passionless one. Before long, he fell madly in love with Sara Hutchison, the sister-in-law of his good friend William Wordsworth (Aries, see page 25). Hutchison rejected his advances, but Coleridge remained a lovelorn mess, writing poem after poem to his beloved "Asra." By all accounts, Sara Hutchison was the polar opposite of Sara Coleridge—warm, hearty, and up for adventure, whereas he described his own wife as cold. Perhaps that coldness had something to do with the fact that she was home with four children while he was pining after his reluctant muse. So was he a humanitarian poet obsessed with equality, or was he an opium-addicted wretch who neglected his kids and relentlessly pursued an uninterested woman? He was a Libra; he could have been both.

Coleridge and Wordsworth ushered in the Romantic Age when they published *Lyrical Ballads* in 1798. In this collection, Coleridge gave us "The Rime of the Ancient Mariner"—a story of a sea voyage gone wrong and all the Libra darkness that accompanies it. Taking the form of a dialogue between a wedding guest and an old seafarer, the poem tells the story of a sea captain who kills an albatross. It is from this poem that we derive the symbol of an albatross around one's neck as a metaphor for being undone by one's own sins. An essentially Libra metaphor, that—externalizing guilt by tarnishing one's outward appearance. Similarly, it is this poem that gave us the oft-misquoted line "water, water, everywhere / Nor any drop to drink," highlighting the Libran ability to hold opposites in comfortable conjunction.

Although Libras tend to gravitate to luxury, Coleridge famously spent time alone in a drafty farmhouse near Somerset where he claims "Kubla Khan" came to him in an opium fever dream. Before he could get the whole thing down, he was interrupted by a "Person from Porlock." This person distracted him with chatter before departing, leaving Coleridge unable to finish the poem. Much fictional use has been made of this mysterious visitor, as authors as disparate as Douglas Adams (Pisces) and Vladimir Nabokov (Taurus) have name-checked him, but no one knows for sure who this interrupter might have been. All we know is that he arrived abruptly without invitation, talked quite a bit, and then left just as suddenly. Given these facts, it is probably safe to assume that he was a Sagittarius. However, only a Libra would have let him inside.

NOTES FOR WRITERS WITH OTHER LIBRA PLACEMENTS

WRITER'S CORNER

POSITIVE ASPECTS

You have an innate ability to find beauty in the mundane and to convey that with a flair for the fantastic.

NEGATIVE ASPECTS

You tend to be indecisive, which can hamper your progress. You might need to set page- or word-count goals to help you focus.

WRITER BEWARE

Partnership is your safe space, but this means you can give away your power. Take constructive criticism but prioritize your own writerly instincts.

LIBRA MOON: Much of this will likely resonate with you on an emotional level. Because Libra rules the 7th House of partnership, Libra Moons have a knack for working well with others. Whether it's in groups or pairs, a Libra Moon might benefit from collaboration.

LIBRA RISING: You often embody the most overt aspects of the sign in a way that is readily visible to others. You have the gift of gab and the ability to entertain a crowd. Consider doing spoken-word poetry or performing your work in front of an audience.

MERCURY IN LIBRA: You have a knack for beauty and a flair for balance. When writing a longer work, you may have an instinctive feeling for plot structure. Trust those instincts.

VENUS IN LIBRA: You are the consummate romantic. Libra rules the house of marriage and is ruled by the goddess of love, making you a prime candidate to write the next great epic love poem or a swoon-worthy page-turner. In a world that needs all the love it can get, you might just have the panacea to bring us all together. Follow that starry-eyed romanticism and see where it takes you.

MARS IN LIBRA: Mars in Libra writers are defenders of the weak and champions of the disenfranchised. You care deeply about social change, and injustice of any kind can upset you deeply. This is what drives you to act. However, you may get so caught up in an idea that you can see both sides, and suddenly your writing may come to a halt. If this is the case, take some time, clear your head, and listen to that inner voice that tells you where you need to go.

TRY THIS!

+ FIND a piece of artwork that you consider truly beautiful (a painting, a piece of music, a video of a dance), and use the joy you get from the piece to inspire a poem or a short story.

+ TAKE two things that don't logically go together and use them as a starting point for a poem.

+ CONSIDER what social issues concern you most. What do you love, and what would you do to protect it? Write a persuasive essay about something that matters deeply to you.

READER'S CORNER
COMPATIBILITY CHART

Which Libra-composed book is most likely to appeal to you? It depends on your sign. Look for your match below. And don't forget to look at your rising and Moon signs if you know those.

SIGN	CLASSIC	MODERN
ARIES	OSCAR WILDE, *The Importance of Being Earnest*	AMBER SMITH, *The Way I Used to Be*
TAURUS	T. S. ELIOT, *The Waste Land*	TRUMAN CAPOTE, *In Cold Blood*
GEMINI	P. G. WODEHOUSE, *The Code of the Woosters*	R. L. STINE, *Fear Street: The New Girl*
CANCER	HORACE WALPOLE, *The Castle of Otranto*	NICOLA YOON, *Everything, Everything*
LEO	LEIGH HUNT, *Complete Works*	BELL HOOKS, *All About Love*
VIRGO	F. SCOTT FITZGERALD, *The Great Gatsby*	URSULA K. LE GUIN, *The Left Hand of Darkness*

SIGN	CLASSIC	MODERN
LIBRA	FRANCES ELLEN WATKINS HARPER, *Iola Leroy*	SHEL SILVERSTEIN, *Where the Sidewalk Ends*
SCORPIO	SAMUEL TAYLOR COLERIDGE, *Collected Works*	ANNE RICE, *The Witching Hour*
SAGITTARIUS	MIGUEL DE CERVANTES, *Don Quixote*	DUNCAN B. BARLOW, *A Dog Between Us*
CAPRICORN	E. E. CUMMINGS, *Tulips and Chimneys*	ROXANE GAY, *Difficult Women*
AQUARIUS	RUMI, *Collected Works*	TA-NEHISI COATES, *Between the World and Me*
PISCES	ARTHUR RIMBAUD, *Collected Works*	NTOZAKE SHANGE, *Liliane*

SCORPIO

SCORPIO

THE SHADOW WRITER

I KNEW NOW WELL ENOUGH WHERE
TO FIND THE MONSTER I SOUGHT.

—Bram Stoker

SCORPIO 101

Scorpios are the deep dark wizards of the zodiac. The denizens of this fixed water sign are like portals that open up into worlds of shadow, intensity, and the beauty of primordial darkness. They are often maligned as villains, but we contend that this is a misapprehension of their singular gifts. Scorpio is perhaps the most misunderstood sign of the zodiac. It's true—they can be drawn to the taboo, the occult, and the ghastly, but this impulse is born out of an admirable curiosity and a willingness to look unflinchingly at the more morbid aspects of reality instead of sweeping them under the rug. Whether we want to acknowledge death, destruction, and suffering or not, these forces still exist. Scorpio is simply brave enough to look them square in the face.

Scorpio rules the 8th House, the house of sex, death, and other people's money. It's concerned with the hidden side of humanity, and as such, that which is concealed has a strong draw for Scorpios. They have no time for superficiality, and because our society tends to thrive on the superficial, a Scorpio can seem a bit like a fish out of water (or a scorpion out of sand) when it comes to situations that require them to remain on the surface. Scorpios want to dive deep. They are natural detectives. Shrouded in mystery themselves, they are pulled to investigate anything that isn't immediately obvious. They can uncover a secret more easily than any other sign, so don't even try to fool a Scorpio. They already see

SIGN OVERVIEW

SYMBOL:
The Scorpion

ELEMENT: Water

QUALITY: Fixed

HOUSE RULED:
8th (Sex, Death,
Other People's Money)

PLANETARY RULER:
Mars/Pluto

POSITIVE TRAITS:
Curious, Formidable,
Honest

NEGATIVE TRAITS:
Possessive, Paranoid,
Controlling

right through you. And yes, they see the bad parts, but that doesn't have to be a bad thing. Astrologer Adam Elenbaas contends that Scorpios are the watchdogs of the zodiac, that their need for control and focus on the moribund is born out of heightened awareness of very real dangers. We can put our heads in the sand all we want, but that doesn't make the evils of the world vanish. Thankfully, while our heads are buried and our bodies are exposed, Scorpios are watching over us like sentinels, unafraid of confronting difficult truths.

In modern times, Pluto has become the co-ruler of Scorpio, and it is from Pluto that Scorpio draws some of its deadlier qualities. But in ancient times, Scorpio, along with Aries, was ruled solely by Mars. The god of war, Mars is primed to go on the attack when under threat. In an Aries, this attack will be obvious, open, and overtly confrontational, but Mars in Scorpio swims in hidden waters. Mars's influence in Scorpio is more recondite. You won't see it coming. It moves through the night under the cover of darkness, and when it attacks, you won't have time to block, much less counterattack. And this is why you don't piss off a Scorpio. It's not an accident that Scorpio's symbol is the scorpion with its formidable armor and legendary stinger. You don't want a Scorpio to sting you, but there is a very simple way to make sure that doesn't happen: be kind to them, treat them with respect, and don't let a superficial understanding of astrology continue to malign this powerful sign.

THE SCORPIO WRITER:
A LITERARY HISTORY

Scorpio poet John Keats begins his great poem *Endymion* with the lines "A thing of beauty is a joy forever: / Its loveliness increases; it will never / Pass into nothingness." The poem continues for about four thousand narrative lines, charting the adventures of a shepherd-prince who, at one point, descends to the underworld. In their pursuit of art that is so beautiful it will never pass into nothingness, Scorpio writers don't hesitate to descend into the depths of human consciousness and to recognize that people, unlike poems, are not immortal. While Keats accomplished this by dwelling with uncertainty, Bram Stoker and Robert Louis Stevenson invented monsters in which we can see ourselves and our worlds in all their darkness and light. Turning to beasts of a gentler kind, we'll consider the work of Marianne Moore, who crafted poems that vibrate like little terrariums, holding life's secrets.

While Taurus is the sign most famous for loyalty, a true bond with a Scorpio, once forged, can survive even the darkest experiences.

CASE STUDY #1: JOHN KEATS

Poetic genius and world-historical sad panda John Keats takes us, in his own quiet way, straight to the heart of the Scorpio experience. Born on Halloween 1795, Keats was joined in quick succession by two younger brothers, George and Tom. Two more siblings followed, a brother (who died) and a sister. Keats left for school and then left school for medical training. Between the years 1814 and 1817, Keats apprenticed to a surgeon-apothecary, then transferred to a hospital where his training included attending lectures by eminent surgeons as well as working in the dissecting room and operating theater. With typical Scorpio competency, Keats remained cool and cerebral under pressure. For example, in March 1816, he saved a woman's life by figuring out the trajectory of a pistol ball using only his knowledge of human anatomy. Keats's poetic activity increased during these years, and it's helpful to understand that his ethereal, mythic, ornate poetry issued not from idleness and daydreaming, but from a working world of hearts and brains, of amputations made necessary by the ravages of war, of life and death. Scorpio writers have a particular emotional intensity that does more than fly away; it roots down into their very blood and bones.

Keats knew many of the Romantic poets through Leigh Hunt (Libra), a radical publisher and writer who gathered a constellation of literary stars around himself. In 1817, Keats moved in with his brothers in Hampstead, near the large, public green space known as Hampstead Heath. There, Keats helped nurse his brother Tom, who was suffering from tuberculosis. Keats left on a walking tour, grew ill, and returned home, where he continued to nurse Tom until his death in 1818. It is likely that, in the act of nursing his brother, Keats exposed himself to the disease that would ultimately kill him as well.

Near the end of his life, Keats, while traveling in Italy for his health, would express in a letter to a friend that he felt he was "leading a posthumous existence." While, by that time, his sense of inhabiting his own afterlife had much to do with his impending death, the idea of being posthumous to oneself runs through some of Keats's most celebrated work, of which a preoccupation with mortality is a hallmark. For example, in "Ode on a Grecian Urn," an immortal object from ancient times stands in stark contrast to the mortal human observer. Describing the scene portrayed on the urn's side, Keats writes:

> Heard melodies are sweet, but those unheard
> Are sweeter; therefore, ye soft pipes, play on;
> Not to the sensual ear, but, more endear'd,
> Pipe to the spirit ditties of no tone:
> Fair youth, beneath the trees, thou canst not leave
> Thy song, nor ever can those trees be bare;
> Bold Lover, never, never canst thou kiss,
> Though winning near the goal yet, do not grieve;
> She cannot fade, though thou hast not thy bliss,
> For ever wilt thou love, and she be fair!

In other words, while a work of art can't hear music or satisfy its desires, it does have time on its side. The nonhuman world of artifice cannot spoil, or die, or fade away. People are mortal, but art, perhaps, is not. And while an image of a lover never quite grasping the object of his affection can never do what a kiss can, it is more solid, less ephemeral, than a kiss could ever be.

Elsewhere in Keats's corpus, he elides sleep with death. In "Ode to a Nightingale," in part a meditation on poetic identity, Keats asks, "Was it a vision, or a waking dream? / Fled is that music:—Do I wake or sleep?" By "Do I wake or sleep," Keats also means, "Am I alive or am I living a posthumous existence?" This bone-deep sense of mortality comes from

Keats's experiences at the operating table and at his brother's bedside, sure, but it also speaks to Scorpio's deep and abiding sense of life's fragility. Indeed, according to one account, Keats left his medical activities quite suddenly. He was sewing an artery back to the heart after surgery, had a moment of vivid sensation in which he understood what would happen if he made the slightest error, came home, and refused to pick up surgical instruments ever again.

YOU MIGHT BE A SCORPIO IF:
you make decisions quickly and then stick to them forever.

Keats's sonnet "When I Have Fears That I May Cease to Be" speaks to the poet's profound awareness of his own mortality and the notion that real, human love can only ever be fleeting in the grand scheme of things:

When I have fears that I may cease to be
Before my pen has gleaned my teeming brain,
Before high-pilèd books, in charactery,
Hold like rich garners the full ripened grain;
When I behold, upon the night's starred face,
Huge cloudy symbols of a high romance,
And think that I may never live to trace
Their shadows with the magic hand of chance;
And when I feel, fair creature of an hour,
That I shall never look upon thee more,
Never have relish in the faery power
Of unreflecting love—then on the shore
Of the wide world I stand alone, and think
Till love and fame to nothingness do sink.

In this poem, Keats elides human mortality with the fleeting nature of everyday moments, such as seeing a pretty face that one might never see again. Love and fame sink in comparison to the weight of human mortality and the passage of time, because recognizing life's fleeting nature renders both difficult, and because life's ephemeral nature threatens to render human experience meaningless.

The idea of a posthumous existence relates to another concept that Keats invented and that has had a profound influence on how people think about poetry. This is the notion of "negative capability." We can't really say that Keats developed this idea, as it appears only once in his writing—in a letter written to his brothers in 1817. There, after complaining about how the shallowness of the artsy, hipster social scene was driving him bananas, Keats claimed to have had an epiphany about what makes a great writer. He defined this as "negative capability," or the quality of being "capable of being in uncertainties, mysteries, doubts, without any irritable reaching after fact & reason." Remember, Scorpios are comfortable embodying and confronting the deep mysteries of life; in fact, for Keats, being comfortable with mysteries was the defining quality of a great writer.

So who didn't have negative capability? According to Keats, Samuel Taylor Coleridge (Libra, see page 164) sure didn't. In his letter to his brothers, Keats wrote, "Coleridge, for instance, would let go by a fine isolated verisimilitude caught from the Penetralium of mystery, from being incapable of remaining content with half-knowledge." Nobody drags an acquaintance quite as artfully as a Scorpio.

Scorpios understand that love and death are deeply connected, and this connection was visceral in Keats's life. As he nursed his dying brother, Keats also became close with Fanny Brawne (Leo), a young woman of keen intelligence with an artistic bent. The pair read and indulged in deep conversation together, and we know Keats penned a great many letters and poems to and for Fanny. But illness was taking its hold, the sense that life was on solid ground was elusive, and a stable future with Fanny always felt just out of reach. In one particularly dark missive to the object of his adoration, Keats wrote, "I have two luxuries to brood over in my walks; your loveliness, and the hour of my death." Keats was tortured knowing he couldn't afford to marry Fanny and tortured again when he had to part from her in search of a warmer climate for his ailing health. When news of Keats's death in Italy reached Fanny in England, she mourned for years, and didn't marry until more than a decade later. If you've ever loved a Scorpio, you know that they're not easily replaced.

CASE STUDY #2: BRAM STOKER

Scorpio theater kid Bram Stoker was born on November 8, 1847, in a seaside suburb of Dublin. He spent much of his childhood bedridden as a result of a mysterious illness but recovered in time to become a prize athlete during his tenure at Trinity College. While his childhood illness didn't seem to have a lasting effect on Stoker's physical capacities throughout his life, it was likely important to the development of his deep imagination. While the Stoker family was privileged enough to stay relatively safe from the cholera epidemic and Great Famine that coincided with little Bram's birth, the horrors lurking just outside the door no doubt influenced his later contributions to the horror genre. For example, Stoker biographer David J. Skal has connected the so-called coffin ships that carried malnourished and diseased Irish emigrants to North America to the spooky, haunted ship that carries Stoker's immortal vampire, Dracula, to England. Scorpios are blessed—or perhaps cursed—with extraordinary memories and can often remember moments from childhood as if they happened yesterday. So it's not a stretch to think that this difficult moment in Irish history, along with traumatic stories Stoker's mother shared with him from her own youth, might have had a profound effect on his art.

Scorpios can be haunted by steel-trap memories.
Release the springs and catch some inspiration instead.

While working in the civil service and moonlighting as a theater critic, Stoker became friendly with Sir Henry Irving (Aquarius), a famous English actor. Irving invited Stoker to run the Lyceum Theatre, and, along with his new bride, a society beauty named Florence Balcombe (Cancer) who was previously courted by Oscar Wilde (Libra, see page 161), Stoker followed this opportunity to London. The gig placed him at the center of London's bustling theater world where he made many famous friends and acquaintances. Stoker was devoted to Irving and went abroad with him on tours. Stoker also became a prolific writer.

Bram Stoker's most enduring novel, *Dracula*, is possibly the most Scorpio book in existence. The young couple at its center, Mina and Jonathan Harker, are trying to make their honest way in the world. To succeed, they have to encounter the world's darkness and injustice, face an immortal monster, experience intense loss, and look evil straight in the face. They also receive a comprehensive education in the petty ways the world works. The monster himself relies on logistics, bureaucracy, the real estate market, and wealth inequality to work his dark designs, and the Harkers, along with their troupe of vampire hunters, must pull rank, spend cash, catch trains, and so forth if they are to defeat him. As Stoker coalesces his band of vampire hunters—including the Harkers, a rugged American, two eccentric doctors, and a nobleman in mourning—two particularly Scorpionic messages emerge: if you want to succeed, you have to see the darkness, and if you want something done right, you'd better do it yourself.

At one moment in the novel, the vampire hunters are gathered around the tomb of Lucy Westenra, a woman many of them loved who was destroyed by Dracula and who has been turned into a vampire herself. After proving to his followers that, unbelievably, their dearly departed Lucy is the creature who has been biting London's children, the eccentric

Doctor Van Helsing brings his collaborators to Lucy's side to lay her soul to rest. Referring to Lucy's fiancé, Van Helsing says, "It will be a blessed hand for her that shall strike the blow that sets her free. To this I am willing; but is there none amongst us who has a better right? Will it be no joy to think of hereafter in the silence of the night when sleep is not: 'It was my hand that sent her to the stars; it was the hand of him that loved her best; the hand that of all she would herself have chosen, had it been to her to choose?'" The character who is narrating this part of the book explains that both Lucy's fiancé and all the characters present see "the infinite kindness which suggested that his should be the hand that would restore Lucy to us as a holy, and not an unholy, memory." Under the doctor's guidance, then, Lucy's fiancé drives the stake through the heart of his deceased beloved, thus freeing her from her fate as an inhuman monster. It's a gruesome scene, one that can be hard to read, really, but it speaks

in a profound way to the nature of Scorpio. Love and death can coexist; indeed, given the human condition, they always already do. It's just up to us whether to see it or not. Perhaps once we see it, we can love even harder.

While Stoker drew on seven years of exacting and painstaking research (get it? Staking?) to write *Dracula*, its ultimate message, much like Stoker himself, remains a mystery. Was Stoker promoting fear of the other or critiquing it? Scorpionic to its core, *Dracula* offers us no easy answer to this question. Rather, it invites us to probe further, to dive into the cool waters of our fear. To look the monster directly in the eyes and ask what it reveals about ourselves.

CASE STUDY #3: ROBERT LOUIS STEVENSON

Remembered for tales including *Treasure Island* and *Strange Case of Dr Jekyll and Mr Hyde*, Robert Louis Stevenson spent his life in search of art, love, and health. Born on November 13, 1850, in Edinburgh, Scotland, the son of a civil engineer who had several gigs building lighthouses, Stevenson spent formative periods of his youth dispatched to gorgeous Scottish Isles, where he found inspiration in both the island landscapes and the sea.

Stevenson was sickly as a child, with a chronic lung ailment he thought was tuberculosis but might have, in fact, had to do with a rare pulmonary ailment. Stevenson started his engineering training but didn't want to follow in his father's footsteps; he studied law but never practiced; and he went on to have a prolific career as a writer, penning travel books, essays, poetry, and novels. His rejection of a more conventional career, as well as his atheism, caused some tension with his father, who nonetheless supported him financially. Even though Stevenson didn't have immediate success and his works were dismissed by some, he would pen masterpieces and inspire literary figures including Jorge Luis Borges (Virgo) and Henry James (Aries).

Stevenson moved often in an effort to find a climate that would support his health, traveling from England to the French Riviera, across America, and to Switzerland and the Scottish Highlands. He spent the last part of his life in the South Seas, dying in Samoa at the age of forty-four. Like Keats, Stevenson lived with an intense awareness of his own eventual or perhaps impending death, a theme that speaks to the Scorpio's deep sense of endings.

Across the various locales where he lived and wrote, Stevenson cut a striking figure. Noticeably skinny and somewhat unusual looking, with a stringy mustache and expressive, penetrating eyes, he took up a bohemian style of dress including longer hair and a velvet coat. J. M. Barrie (Taurus, see page 49) described his legendary, brilliant conversation as infused with an "indescribable charm." While Scorpios may not be for everybody, they can certainly dazzle when you take them on their own terms.

While in France in 1876, Stevenson met and fell in love with Fanny Osbourne (Pisces), an American woman who was traveling with her children far from the confines of her deteriorating marriage. Fanny would eventually leave her husband to be with Stevenson, though historians are divided regarding whether she was in love with or taking advantage of him. Stevenson worked hard to support Fanny and her children, sometimes writing from his sickbed. The couple eventually settled in Samoa, where Stevenson continued writing and became active in local politics. When Stevenson passed away suddenly, most likely of a brain hemorrhage, he was buried overlooking the sea.

In *Strange Case of Dr Jekyll and Mr Hyde*, Stevenson participated in the Gothic revival trend that included such works as Bram Stoker's *Dracula* and Oscar Wilde's *The Picture of Dorian Gray*. *Jekyll and Hyde* quickly became a craze, garnering readers in both England and the United States and inspiring a stage adaptation. The story of a scientist who dabbles in the dark side and manages to bring out his evil alter ego, with disastrous results, *Jekyll and Hyde* explores the duality of human nature and the dark underbelly of the human experience. With unflinching Scorpio honesty, Stevenson developed a monster narrative about a scientist who doesn't create an external being, like Mary Shelley's (Virgo, see page 131) Frankenstein, but instead unleashes the monster within. The implication here is that there is a monster within us all.

YOU MIGHT BE A SCORPIO IF:

nobody forgets that they've met you.

I smiled, comparing myself with other
men, comparing my active goodwill with
the lazy cruelty of their neglect. And
at the very moment of that vainglorious
thought, a qualm came over me, a horrid
nausea and the most deadly shuddering.
These passed away, and left me faint;
and then as in its turn the faintness sub-
sided, I began to be aware of a change
in the temper of my thoughts, a greater
boldness, a contempt of danger, a solu-
tion of the bonds of obligation. I looked
down; my clothes hung formlessly on my
shrunken limbs; the hand that lay on my
knee was corded and hairy. I was once
more Edward Hyde. A moment before
I had been safe of all men's respect,
wealthy, beloved—the cloth laying for me
in the dining room at home; and now
I was the common quarry of mankind,
hunted, houseless, a known murderer,
thrall to the gallows.

While Scorpios have long been maligned for pointing this out, their
willingness to see our darker edges doesn't make them any worse than
the rest of us. It only means they have a heightened awareness and the
courage to tell the truth about human nature.

CODA: MARIANNE MOORE

Born toward the end of the nineteenth century—on November 15, 1887, to be exact—Marianne Moore was an American poet who brought to her formally complex poetry a sense of animality and intrigue. Born in Missouri, she soon moved to Pennsylvania, then attended Bryn Mawr College, where she crossed paths with fellow modernist poet H.D. (Virgo). Moore made her way to the avant-garde literary scene of New York's Greenwich Village, where her poems were admired by American literary heavyweights including Ezra Pound (Scorpio), William Carlos Williams (Virgo), H.D., T. S. Eliot (Libra), and, later, Wallace Stevens (Libra). Celebrated in her life as a stellar poet, Moore would go on to become a bit of a literary celebrity, known for her tricorn hat and cape (as we are seeing, Scorpio writers may have the tendency to develop a signature look).

In a famous poem called "Poetry," Moore suggests that poems should have "imaginary gardens with real toads in them." This statement gets to the heart of the matter when it comes to Scorpio writing. These writers may take us on flights of fancy, across sweeping, epic poems, into the make-believe entrapments of chilling Gothic tales, or across the globe on adventurous travels and in search of treasure. But in the end, their stories tell us about the real world—imperfect, full of problems, but beautiful nonetheless.

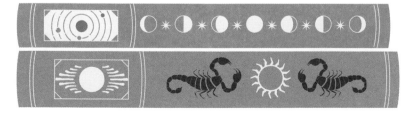

NOTES FOR WRITERS WITH OTHER SCORPIO PLACEMENTS

WRITER'S CORNER

POSITIVE ASPECTS

You have a natural understanding of the depths of human nature. Use this to create starkly realistic characters.

NEGATIVE ASPECTS

Your interest in the hidden realms of the human psyche can lead to paranoia at times. Maintain a sense of balance in your writing.

WRITER BEWARE

Just because you can see through other people doesn't mean you have to pay attention to them. Keep your focus on your own work to avoid distraction.

SCORPIO MOON: You're an intensely private person. You've a powerful capacity for sustained concentration, and you're capable of tremendous depth in your writing. However, you may have difficulty with projects that infringe upon your need for privacy. Don't feel pressured in this sphere. We may live in the world of the tell-all memoir, but push back against provocations to share more of your inner world than you're comfortable sharing.

SCORPIO RISING: You have the capacity to be something of a visionary leader. Brilliant ideas seem to come to you out of the shadowy depths of your Plutonian waters, and others are drawn to your hypnotic oratory powers. Giving readings of your work could potentially garner you something of a cult following. You are capable of accomplishing pretty much anything you set your mind to, so use those powers for good.

MERCURY IN SCORPIO: You are the natural detective of the zodiac. Your innate skill at uncovering the truth and exposing secrets makes you a phenomenal researcher. You can discover things that no one else can. Perhaps you're drawn to heady nonfiction, or some intensely accurate historical fiction. Whatever genre calls to you, you're certain to uncover its depths. Get thee to an archive!

VENUS IN SCORPIO: You're capable of painting luminous, sensual scenes that get to the very heart of what it means to be in love. More than perhaps any other sign, you've a gift for writing erotica, should you choose to use it. The depths of your passions mixed with your immense creativity could translate to some serious fireworks on the page.

MARS IN SCORPIO: You're the very picture of determination. Once you set your mind to accomplishing a project, nothing will stand in your way. Deeply affected by your emotions, but not necessarily expressive of them, your writing can hold a powerful, passionate intensity. You're not afraid of looking death in the face and challenging it to a duel. Better to do this in your writing than in real life, though.

TRY THIS!

+ THINK of something that scares you. Now write a poem or story inspired by this fear that never mentions the fear itself.

+ SET a timer for five minutes and try to write without stopping until the alarm goes off. Begin with the prompt "I may never know." Any time you reach a stopping point, return to this prompt until your time is up.

+ WRITE a monster narrative inspired by a story you've been seeing in the news.

READER'S CORNER:
COMPATIBILITY CHART

Which Scorpio-composed book is most likely to appeal to you? It depends on your sign. Look for your match below. And don't forget to look at your rising and Moon signs if you know those.

SIGN	CLASSIC	MODERN
ARIES	ROBERT LOUIS STEVENSON, *Kidnapped*	MARJANE SATRAPI, *Persepolis*
TAURUS	JOHN KEATS, *The Odes*	YIYUN LI, *Dear Friend, from My Life I Write to You in Your Life*
GEMINI	CHINUA ACHEBE, *Things Fall Apart*	CAMILLE DEANGELIS, *Mary Modern*
CANCER	SYLVIA PLATH, *The Collected Poems*	NEIL GAIMAN, *Fragile Things*
LEO	DYLAN THOMAS, *The Collected Poems*	CARLOS FUENTES, *Where the Air Is Clear*
VIRGO	FYODOR DOSTOEVSKY, *Crime and Punishment*	KAZUO ISHIGURO, *Never Let Me Go*

SIGN	CLASSIC	MODERN
LIBRA	ALBERT CAMUS, *The Plague*	KURT VONNEGUT, *Hocus Pocus*
SCORPIO	ANNE SEXTON, *The Complete Poems*	DON DELILLO, *The Body Artist*
SAGITTARIUS	EVELYN WAUGH, *Brideshead Revisited*	SHARON OLDS, *Stag's Leap*
CAPRICORN	OLIVER GOLDSMITH, *The Vicar of Wakefield*	MICHAEL CRICHTON, *Dragon Teeth*
AQUARIUS	BRAM STOKER, *Dracula*	MARY GAITSKILL, *Veronica*
PISCES	JOHN BERRYMAN, *The Dream Songs*	JOS CHARLES, *Feeld*

+ SAGITTARIUS +

SAGITTARIUS

THE WRITER WHO CHARTS THEIR OWN COURSE

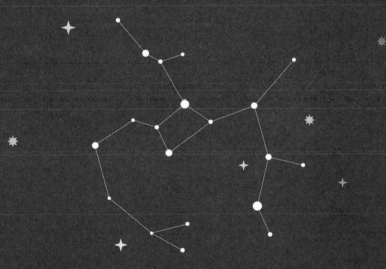

IF I FEEL PHYSICALLY AS IF THE TOP OF MY HEAD
WERE TAKEN OFF, I KNOW THAT IS POETRY.

—Emily Dickinson

SAGITTARIUS 101

Sagittarius is the wild adventurer of the zodiac. They have a reputation for being rebels and party animals (and far be it from us to disagree), but there is a lot more to this maverick than empty beer cans spilling out of ATVs.

A mutable fire sign, Sagittarius is symbolized by the archer or the centaur. Like the Geminian twins and the two Piscean fish, Sagittarius is a double-bodied sign. Every Sagittarius is two beings at once. Half human, half horse, a Sagittarius embodies the highest aspects of the human intellect as well as the most base and rowdy aspects of the centaur's animal nature. They have a knack for excess and a liveliness that would shame even the most intemperate partier, but they are also the essence of erudition.

In some traditions, Sagittarius is represented by the centaur Chiron, the wise teacher who trained such luminaries as Achilles and Odysseus. Gifted at medicine, music, and prophecy, Chiron was also considered the father of botany, and his gentle, kindly nature separated him from his raucous brethren. Chiron is also known as the wounded healer; though he was phenomenally skilled with medicine, when he was struck by a poison arrow, he was tragically unable to heal himself. Similarly, a Sagittarius often brings a boisterous healing energy into every situation, but they can neglect their own deeper healing needs. Blessed with an impulsive streak that puts all other signs to shame, they can sometimes leap before they look and, missing their target, fall straight onto that poison arrow.

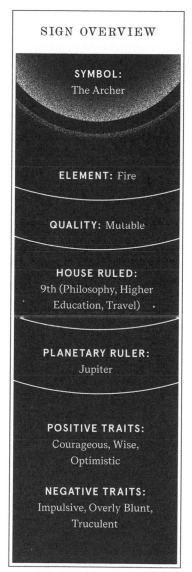

SIGN OVERVIEW

SYMBOL:
The Archer

ELEMENT: Fire

QUALITY: Mutable

HOUSE RULED:
9th (Philosophy, Higher
Education, Travel)

PLANETARY RULER:
Jupiter

POSITIVE TRAITS:
Courageous, Wise,
Optimistic

NEGATIVE TRAITS:
Impulsive, Overly Blunt,
Truculent

Sagittarius rules the 9th House of philosophy, travel, and higher education, and many a Sagittarius can lecture with the best of them. While their opposite sign, Gemini, rules minute, trivial knowledge, Sagittarius rules larger concepts and philosophy. They can often wear the mantle of the sage of the zodiac, but a sage who might not always listen to their own advice.

Jupiter is the planetary ruler of Sagittarius, and while this Benefic endows the sign with its optimism and good luck, the planet is also responsible for Sagittarius's legendary honesty. The thing about honesty is that most people claim to value it, but they only do so up to a point. There is a line where honesty shifts into insult, and wherever that line is for you, Sagittarius is bound to cross it. They mean well. They are buoyed forth on the waves of their own expansive ideals, and they will tell you the hard truths, even if it may sting just a little. They tell it like it is because they think it's best that everyone know the truth up front rather than get irretrievably crushed by it somewhere down the line.

Jupiter may be the bringer of luck and abundance, but he's also a bit of an obnoxious reveler at times, and under the worst of circumstances, a Sagittarius can descend into something of a chaos creator. It may look like charming chaos at first, but it's all fun and games until a centaur puts your eye out. Jupiter also gifts Sagittarius with immense generosity—a generosity that can sometimes be mistaken for hedonism. A Sagittarius will never close the door to a stranger in need. Nor will they close it on the stranger who simply wants to have a good time. The next thing you know, an extravagant bacchanal is in full swing and, well, it may actually look a lot like hedonism, but it is hedonism born of benevolence. We recommend sitting back, enjoying the party, and hoping things calm down a bit tomorrow.

THE SAGITTARIUS WRITER:
A LITERARY HISTORY

If nineteenth-century literature had a Sun sign, it well might be Sagittarius. From William Blake and Emily Dickinson's paradigm-shifting experiments in form and perspective to Jane Austen, George Eliot, and Mark Twain's embrace of the novel genre to capture the complexities of real life to Louisa May Alcott and Dorothy Wordsworth's creative interpretations of domestic experience, the archer's capacious bow sent arrows of innovation and expression far across the nineteenth-century literary landscape.

A Sagittarius will sometimes see the world a little . . . differently.
Sags have a unique ability to catch the sparkles bouncing off our everyday reality. If you love a Sagittarius, let them stop and look, then listen as they describe in vivid detail the moss on the side of a stone or a figure hidden in the architecture. Don't let that light go out.

CASE STUDY #1: WILLIAM BLAKE

Multimedia badass William Blake—a poet, painter, and engraver—had a divine Sagittarian spark that coursed through the brilliant products of his experimental methods. Born November 28, 1757, in Soho, London, to a family of moderate means, the young Blake was always in touch with his mystical nature. As a boy, Blake claimed to have seen "bright angelic wings bespangling every bough like stars" in a tree and "angelic figures walking" in a field among workers as they gathered in the hay. His visionary consciousness was one of the strands by which he connected himself to literary history. For example, in a later work devoted to his literary idol and fellow Sagittarius John Milton, Blake writes about Milton's spirit descending into his garden and entering Blake's body through his left foot, thereby joining the two poets in inspiration.

Blake went to drawing school at the age of ten. When he was fourteen, his parents decided to apprentice him to a master engraver instead, as the cost of continued artistic training was prohibitive. Blake rejected the first engraver they brought him to, saying, "I do not like the man's face: It looks as if he will live to be hanged!" The man would in fact be hanged twelve years later. Luckily, the next engraver Blake considered, James Basire (Libra), had a more appealing visage. As part of Blake's work duties, Basire sent him to spend time in Westminster Abbey drawing monuments that Basire had been commissioned to engrave. Time among the Gothic architecture, looming monuments, and awe-inspiring religious iconography of Westminster Abbey was fruitful to Blake's imaginative development.

At twenty-one, Blake left his apprenticeship. He enrolled in the newly formed Royal Academy of Arts but made his living engraving illustrations for various publications. Around this time, Blake witnessed riots in London provoked by several causes, including protest against further war with the American colonies. He would later channel these scenes of rage, destruction, cruelty, and chaos to make his original work very punk rock.

Blake's etched frontispiece for *Europe: a Prophecy.*

New York Public Library Digital Collections

Blake married Catherine Boucher (Taurus), a kind beauty who couldn't write her own name. He taught her to read and write and she became an invaluable draftsman and assistant to him. Though ultimately childless, the marriage was happy, collaborative, and even whimsical—according to one story, an acquaintance once happened upon Blake and his wife naked in the garden, reading Milton's *Paradise Lost* aloud in character as Adam and Eve. Blake's career in printing and connection to radical publishing also brought him into contact with thinkers including Henry Fuseli (Aquarius), Mary Wollstonecraft (Taurus, see page 44), and Thomas Paine (Aquarius).

In 1787, Blake's beloved younger brother, Robert, passed away after an illness. Blake tended to his brother tirelessly in his final weeks and, in his grief and exhaustion, claimed to see "the released spirit ascend heavenward, clapping its hands for joy." Blake felt that his brother's spirit lived with him and that he could communicate with it. He even claimed that Robert taught him his experimental method of illuminated writing.

This original printing method, which Blake invented, is perhaps the most Sagittarian artistic practice imaginable. You see, per the standard method of the time, engraving involved a time-consuming process. The copper plate was prepared with an acid-resistant film and then the design was engraved with a needle in order to expose the plate's surface to acid, which bit the design into the copper. Blake inverted this process, employing a relief etching method. Instead of protecting the entire plate from acid and then making a series of exacting marks to burn in the design, Blake's method involved painting the design directly onto the plate using an acid-resistant varnish. When acid was applied, what hadn't been painted would burn away. In other words, Blake painted his revelations directly onto the plate and burned all falsehoods away with acid. This practice of revelation by fire is Sagittarian to its core. Remember, Sagittarius values honesty at all costs. The resulting prints were then hand-colored, offering further opportunities for artistic flair.

In his illuminated book *The Marriage of Heaven and Hell*, Blake describes this process as "printing in the infernal method, by corrosives, which in Hell are salutary and medicinal, melting apparent surfaces away, and displaying the infinite which was hid."

Blake goes on to write that "If the doors of perception were cleansed every thing would appear to man as it is: infinite." A Sagittarius genius ahead of his time, Blake experienced his revelatory visions, painted them on metal (again, he was metal as hell), and destroyed whatever crap was hiding the truth. Count on a Sagittarius to see things in a fresh light . . . and to leave their mark in an unusual way.

That Blake quote above, about the doors of perception?
That's where the band The Doors got their name.
(Jim Morrison was also a Sagittarius.)

Another famous collection of Blake's work, *Songs of Innocence and of Experience*, complicates the dual nature of life. Indeed, some of the "songs of innocence" are just as dark and tragic as their more experienced counterparts. For example, in "The Chimney Sweeper," Blake offers a damning portrayal of the way the promise of salvation was used to oppress children. In the poem, a boy named Tom has a dream: "That thousands of sweepers Dick, Joe, Ned & Jack / Were all of them lock'd up in coffins of black, / And by came an Angel who had a bright key, / And he open'd the coffins & set them all free." Based on this vision, Tom is able to go about his life of grueling child labor cheerfully, placing his hope in the next world: "And so Tom awoke and we rose in the dark / And got with our bags & our brushes to work. / Tho' the morning was cold, Tom was happy & warm. / So if all do their duty, they need not fear harm." If this is a song of innocence, then it is a song of innocence as victimhood, as naivete, or simply as plain helplessness under systems of injustice and oppression. Rather than offer innocence as inspiration, *Songs of Innocence and of Experience* suggests that innocence in an unjust world is not so different from experience, after all. Here Blake uses the complex nature of poetry to share a child's worldview sweetly and respectfully while revealing the truth about that worldview, namely that it has been inculcated in the child to serve the powers that be. Sagittarius writers are powerful truth tellers, not only in their ability to represent reality in their writing, but also in their ability to provoke revelations about things taken for granted that might in fact be deeply unfair.

CASE STUDY #2: JANE AUSTEN

It's possible nobody really knew who Jane Austen was, besides her sister, best friend, and first reader, Cassandra (Capricorn). Accordingly, Austen's works are dappled with pairs of tight-knit sisters, such as Lizzy and Jane in *Pride and Prejudice* and Elinor and Marianne in *Sense and Sensibility.* (Remember, Sagittarius is a double-bodied sign.)

We do know that Austen was born on December 16, 1775, a clergyman's daughter, and that she and Cassandra, along with their brothers, grew up in a country parsonage in the village of Steventon, Hampshire. We know Jane and Cassandra spent some time together away at school— Jane leaving for school earlier than was appropriate, rather than facing separation from her sister. A prolific reader and writer from a young age, Austen produced cutting, witty juvenilia, much of which displays her engagement with the dark, Gothic novels that were all the rage during this period as well as with other popular fiction devoured as a child in her father's library. In Austen's youthful writing, characters poison their nemeses and kick one another out of windows. The juvenilia is fascinating both for its quick, youthful wit and because it gives us a sense of Austen's influences, which included popular fiction.

According to Austen scholar Stephanie Insley Hershinow, Cassandra and the Austen family in general were supportive of her writing—her father gave her a portable writing desk, her brother accompanied her to London to help her negotiate the world of publishing, and her nieces and nephews were delighted with her early works. Despite this support, Austen did not publish a novel until 1811, only six years before her death.

After Jane Austen's death, her family cultivated an image of her as the ideal, content, unmarried woman, or "Aunt Jane," an image that Austen scholar Devoney Looser argues has persisted across generations of Austen fandom. "One near constant," Looser writes, "is that her imagined intimacy with audiences has been described as of the coziest, quotidian, familial kind." Despite this coziness, Austen certainly knew her share of instability and displacement. Her father entrusted his income to his son in 1801, moving the family to Bath; Austen would critique the superficiality of the Bath social scene in novels including *Northanger Abbey* and *Persuasion*. Some say that, following the move to Bath, Austen fell in love with a clergyman who died shortly after; Cassandra's fiancé died young as well.

In 1802, Austen received an offer of marriage from her friend's brother, Harris Bigg-Wither. Bigg-Wither, who was visiting his sisters, was heir to an estate back in Hampshire, and probably represented Austen's only chance at a home of her own, one in which she could likely have housed her mother and sister following her father's death. Due to the custom of leaving land and wealth to an eldest son or sometimes daughter, Austen must have known that poverty and dependence on others threatened if she or her sister did not marry well. She accepted

Bigg-Wither's proposal, then changed her mind the next day, later explaining to her niece that "Anything is to be preferred or endured rather than marrying without Affection." Austen biographer Lucy Worsley supposes that Bigg-Wither simply did not appeal: "Although there was nothing terribly wrong with him, he was described as being 'awkward, & even uncouth in manner.' There really was little 'but his size to recommend him.'" (These are quotes from a relative, not from Austen herself.) While it's certainly extremely possible that there's some crucial detail to this story of which we are simply not aware (notably, Cassandra censored her sister's letters after her death, omitting, among other things, any mention of her one-night engagement), it's worth mentioning that accepting an engagement and then changing your mind, let alone passing on security because it doesn't make your soul sing, is very Sag.

In a fate that many of Austen's heroines experience, or fear, her father's death in 1805 left Austen essentially homeless (although it did, as she put it, offer an "escape" from Bath). Along with her mother and sister, Austen stayed with friends and relations in various places until her brother Edward, who had been adopted as heir by a relative, created a cottage home for them at Chawton. While Austen's initial dealings with the publishing industry were rather frustrating, she eventually began publishing novels toward the end of her life, with some of her major works appearing only posthumously.

You MIGHT be a Sagittarius IF: whatever you do, you go hard. Hobbies quickly become expensive as you collect all the best equipment and sometimes even morph into small businesses when your casual creations are so spectacular that the whole world wants a piece.

Alas! if the heroine of one novel be not patronized by the
heroine of another, from whom can she expect protection and
regard? I cannot approve of it. Let us leave it to the Reviewers
to abuse such effusions of fancy at their leisure, and over every
new novel to talk in threadbare strains of the trash with which
the press now groans. Let us not desert one another;
we are an injured body.

—*NORTHANGER ABBEY*

Perhaps more than any nineteenth-century novelist, Jane Austen
wrote her star chart. With its humble but determined heroine standing
her moral ground and insisting on her own self-belonging in the face of
social corruption, declarations of love, and insidious leisure, *Mansfield
Park* issued straight from Austen's Virgo ascendant. With its emphasis on
the romance of setting things right, no matter how much time has passed,
Persuasion sings to Austen's Capricorn Mars and Libran Saturn and Moon.
With their doubling, twinning, and world-creating chatter, *Emma* and
Sense and Sensibility both speak to Jupiter and Uranus in Gemini, while
the meta-Gothic edges of both *Northanger Abbey* and *Lady Susan* let Austen's Venus in Scorpio shine. But nowhere is Austen's Sagittarian nature
(Sun and Mercury) on fuller display than in that canonical tale of two outdoorsy hotties who love being super intense about their friendships, opinions, and hobbies but hate doing what they're told, and who change their
minds about each other until they eventually get married: *Pride and Prejudice*. Perhaps from now on we should refer to it as *Pride and Sagittarius*.

Pride and Prejudice offers us a hero and a heroine who both embody
the sign. Lizzy Bennet, smart and sly, loves a laugh and doesn't shy away
from a long walk, even if it means she might muddy her petticoats. When
she is insulted by Darcy at a ball, she takes pleasure in repeating the ridiculous story of the slight to her friends. She has the courage to reject two

proposals, both of which would offer security, but also shows the flexibility to change her mind about Darcy, grow to love him, and accept him when he asks for her hand again. Darcy, for his part, comes off as a bit of a mansplainer but is actually very capable of learning from his mistakes and making amends. By bending and setting the things he messed up to rights, he's able to win Lizzy's heart. Sometimes Sagittarius's stereotypical indecision has a silver lining, as when Sags are able to admit that they were wrong and chart a different course.

CASE STUDY #3: EMILY DICKINSON

Great American poet Emily Dickinson was born on December 10, 1830. Her father was a lawyer and politician active in civic work, and her family owned a homestead in and had deep ties to the local community of Amherst, Massachusetts. Emily had a sister, Lavinia (Pisces), nicknamed "Vinnie," and a brother, William Austin (Aries), who went by Austin. Dickinson attended a local school connected to Amherst College, receiving an expansive education that included the ability to attend college lectures. Her time at school stoked Dickinson's interest in plants and love of the natural world. Dickinson moved on to Mount Holyoke Female Seminary but stayed for only one year, perhaps in part because the religiosity of seminary clashed with her personal views. Returning home signaled an abrupt transition for Dickinson, one that took her from the life of the mind to the housework and frequent social responsibilities of an unmarried daughter. Participating in social visits was not her cup of tea, and she would eventually stop doing so, sticking to baking bread and tending the garden as far as household chores were concerned. Scholar Judith Farr notes that during her life, Dickinson was perhaps more well known as a gardener than as a poet, for she applied her botanical studies to the tending of the homestead garden and created an impressive record of pressed specimens in her herbarium. While Dickinson is often remembered as a mysterious recluse (someone the town children called "the myth"), it is also possible that, by refusing to see most people, she was simply reclaiming her time.

One aspect of Dickinson's life that does remain eminently mysterious is her relationship to her sister-in-law, Susan Gilbert. We know that Sue's marriage to Austin was not a happy or successful one and that Emily eventually facilitated her brother's extramarital affair. We also know that many of Dickinson's poems were written as epistles to Susan. Dickinson's letters to Susan were intensely passionate, but her letters to her female friends were passionate in general. Whether we choose to read the relationship between Dickinson and her Susie as one of intense and sometimes fraught platonic friendship or whether we want to draw on the multitude of evidence to suggest that they were in love, one thing is certain: an artsy Sagittarius can create prolifically when they have a beloved audience of one.

> Wild nights—Wild nights!
> Were I with thee
> Wild nights should be
> Our luxury!
> Futile—the winds -
> To a Heart in port -
> Done with the Compass -
> Done with the Chart!
> Rowing in Eden -
> Ah—the Sea!
> Might I but moor—tonight—
> In thee!

Dickinson's poetry is so defiant of expectation, it still reads as completely and totally fresh even generations after her death. While Dickinson published only ten poems and a letter during her lifetime, she often sent poetry in letters to friends, sometimes enclosed with an artifact such as a dried flower or cricket. When she died, Dickinson left behind a cache of almost 1,800 poems, many of which were sewn into homemade books. Susan also had more than three hundred poems, which had been included in letters. The long process of editing and re-editing Dickinson's work, publishing and republishing it, began with her family. And the question of how to represent her sprawling corpus, which was in part shaped by ephemeral forms, challenges editors to this day.

As we think of Dickinson's buzzing legacy, which flits from flower to flower, perhaps we would do well to sit with one of her poems:

> Fame is a bee.
> It has a song—
> It has a sting—
> Ah, too, it has a wing.

AURORA BOREALIS.

CODA: GEORGE ELIOT, LOUISA MAY ALCOTT, MARK TWAIN, AND DOROTHY WORDSWORTH

Writing under the pen name George Eliot, Mary Ann (Marian) Evans (born November 22, 1819) penned classic novels including *Adam Bede*, *The Mill on the Floss*, *Silas Marner*, and *Middlemarch*, making her one of the most influential English novelists of all time. Often regarded as her masterwork, *Middlemarch* touches on a broad range of historical, social, and psychological issues, integrating them with the plight of its heroine. Mark Twain (born November 30, 1835) similarly integrated broad historical trends into the novel form. *Adventures of Huckleberry Finn*, sometimes called the "Great American Novel," is both a riveting tale of boyhood adventure and a meditation on the cruelty and hypocrisy of slavery. Louisa May Alcott (born November 29, 1832) wrote *Little Women*, a classic of children's literature, while challenging the constraints of femininity, both in her life and in her work. And, by writing her evocative descriptions of home, nature, and daily life in the often literal margins of literary history, famed diarist Dorothy Wordsworth (born December 25, 1771) reminds us that there is an intimate, personal side to even the grandest stories.

NOTES FOR WRITERS WITH OTHER SAGITTARIUS PLACEMENTS

WRITER'S CORNER

POSITIVE ASPECTS

You are honest and brave, and this means you can create absolute wonders with your writing. Don't let anything hold you back!

NEGATIVE ASPECTS

You can be a tad impulsive. Make sure to proofread before you submit something important.

WRITER BEWARE

You have a gift for teaching, but that can sometimes make you a little long-winded and/or mansplainy. If people's eyes start to glaze over, tone it down.

SAGITTARIUS MOON: Your emotions need an outlet, and a lot of the time that outlet may involve physicality or travel. You would do well to try a far-flung writing retreat or to steal away to write while on vacation. You like to live out loud and rarely keep your opinions to yourself. There is a bravery to this that can infuse your writing with an enviable authenticity.

SAGITTARIUS RISING: You don't just walk into a room, you burst through the swinging doors and the patrons in the saloon greet you with a round of hurrahs! Erudite to the extreme, you are gifted with a love of knowledge and a flair for teaching. Your abiding love for your fellow humans serves your keenly drawn character depictions and your ability to charm an interested editor. Your impulsiveness, however, can sometimes mean you get a little bit ahead of yourself. Slow down before you burn some potential bridges.

MERCURY IN SAGITTARIUS: If you are a writer with Mercury in Sagittarius, the words most likely flow quickly and easily from your proverbial pen. Your writing can tend to the experimental; you simply don't like having to follow rules. If someone tells you there is only one way to write, you will immediately do the opposite. This means that you can create absolute magic.

VENUS IN SAGITTARIUS: You may have a gift for translation. You are drawn to travel and might find yourself in distant locales, smitten with the locals, and feasting on their most epicurean delights. You may even consider travel or food writing as a possible genre.

MARS IN SAGITTARIUS: You have a brashness to your writing that is likely to draw in oodles of fans. Mars in Sagittarius writers are the ones found out in the midst of the battlefield, balancing a typewriter on their knees and taking swigs from a bottle of whiskey as bullets whiz past. You have no compunction about telling it like it is, which sometimes gets you into trouble, though there is never even a modicum of cruelty to your truth-telling.

TRY THIS!

+ WRITE a poem constrained by a small piece of paper, like the back of an envelope or a receipt.

+ KEEP a journal connected in some way to nature. This could be a diary of the weather, notes about your garden, or a place where you document the landscapes you encounter in your travels.

+ TRY an erasure poem. Choose a favorite literary text, a text that has special meaning to you, or a text you encounter every day. Using white paper strips or a dark marker, "erase" most of the text, leaving a new poem visible.

READER'S CORNER:
COMPATIBILITY CHART

Which Sagittarius-composed book is most likely to appeal to you? It depends on your sign. Look for your match below. And don't forget to look at your rising and Moon signs if you know those.

SIGN	CLASSIC	MODERN
ARIES	JOAN DIDION, *Slouching Towards Bethlehem*	ARUNDHATI ROY, *The God of Small Things*
TAURUS	DOROTHY WORDSWORTH, *The Grasmere Journals*	TOMMY PICO, *Nature Poem*
GEMINI	GEORGE ELIOT, *Middlemarch*	MORGAN PARKER, *There Are More Beautiful Things Than Beyoncé*
CANCER	EMILY DICKINSON, *The Gorgeous Nothings*	ALEX DIMITROV, *Love and Other Poems*
LEO	WILLIAM BLAKE, *The Book of Urizen*	PHILIP K. DICK, *Do Androids Dream of Electric Sheep?*
VIRGO	JOHN MILTON, *Paradise Lost*	ANN PATCHETT, *Commonwealth*

SIGN	CLASSIC	MODERN
LIBRA	MARK TWAIN, *Adventures of Huckleberry Finn*	GEORGE SAUNDERS, *Lincoln in the Bardo*
SCORPIO	WILLA CATHER, *My Mortal Enemy*	NAGUIB MAHFOUZ, *Heart of the Night*
SAGITTARIUS	JANE AUSTEN, *Pride and Prejudice*	T. C. BOYLE, *Tooth and Claw*
CAPRICORN	JANE AUSTEN, *Mansfield Park*	SAEED JONES, *Prelude to Bruise*
AQUARIUS	SHIRLEY JACKSON, *We Have Always Lived in the Castle*	SANDRA CISNEROS, *The House on Mango Street*
PISCES	EUGENE IONESCO, *Present Past Past Present*	HELEN OYEYEMI, *Boy, Snow, Bird*

✦ **CAPRICORN** ✦

CAPRICORN

THE MYSTERIOUS WRITER

I AM NOT A CLASSICIST NOR A REALIST, IN THE USUAL
SENSE OF THESE TERMS. I AM AN ESSENTIALIST.

—Jean Toomer

CAPRICORN 101

Capricorns are often maligned as the bossy, obstinate patriarchs of the zodiac, obsessed with power and only caring about financial gain. What this interpretation misses, though, is the fundamentally mysterious nature of the sign. In fact, two of the most influential mystery writers of all time were born under this sign. Capricorns are no more the bossy devils of the zodiac than Pisces are the saints. However, some of their supposedly malignant qualities (obsession, calculation, power) are the tools Capricorns use to accomplish the often flabbergasting feats of which they are capable.

Capricorn is an earth sign ruled by the planet Saturn, the notorious disciplinarian of the zodiac. Saturn makes the rules and he enjoys enforcing them. Also, sometimes he eats a child or two. You don't want to mess with Saturn. What's more, Capricorn is the sign in which Mars is exalted, or especially potent. This means that Capricorn is home to not just one, but two planetary Malefics. It's no wonder there is a heaviness to this sign that can sometimes be challenging for more ethereal sorts to grasp. According to myth, it was prophesied that one of Saturn's sons would usurp him, so out of what could glibly be called an abundance of caution, he ate each of his children upon their birth. This is the ruler watching over Capricorn. Whereas Leo sits under the heartening glow of the Sun and Taurus basks in Venus's eternal love, Capricorns have Saturn on their

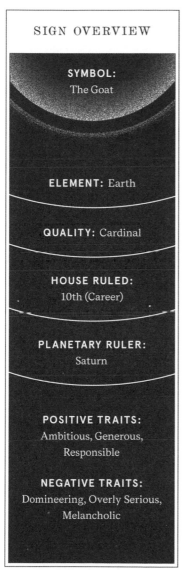

SIGN OVERVIEW

SYMBOL:
The Goat

ELEMENT: Earth

QUALITY: Cardinal

HOUSE RULED:
10th (Career)

PLANETARY RULER:
Saturn

POSITIVE TRAITS:
Ambitious, Generous,
Responsible

NEGATIVE TRAITS:
Domineering, Overly Serious,
Melancholic

case from day one. Sometimes Capricorns can seem almost as if they're carrying the weight of the world on their shoulders. They can be like children who grow up too quickly, gentle dreamers trapped in a world so heavy they are forced to grow mighty horns with which to protect themselves.

Add to this cocktail Mars's warlike influence, and is it any wonder Capricorns feel the need to err on the side of responsibility? Capricorn rules the 10th House of the career. This house is associated with ambition, success, power, and the mark we leave on the world. In many ways, Capricorn's placement in this house is its saving grace. The 10th House is a positive one, and whereas the sign could feel bogged down by all the doom and gloom of its Saturn and Mars relationships, its rulership over the 10th House gives it hope. It is here that Capricorn locates its notorious drive for success. They came into this world with an understanding that life isn't always fair and that the cream doesn't always rise to the top. With both Mars and Saturn looking over their shoulders, they are under no delusion that life is going to be easy.

But the secret is that this cold realism often hides a softer side that Capricorns are reluctant to show. For inside every one of these competitive ascetics is a sensitive artist trying to understand what it all means.

As much as Capricorn can manifest itself in the guise of the patriarch, it is equally liable to come to fruition as a black sheep or hermit. But where the Pisces archetypal hermit might withdraw from society to quietly dream and create art, our Capricorn hermits are as apt to do so because of gambling debts, addiction, or, as is the case with one of our literary Caps, a singular focus on the macabre.

Capricorn is a juxtaposition of calculation and generosity, of despair and hope. This dichotomous nature offers the very thing a Capricorn needs to succeed. There is a heady sort of magic to this sign that makes for haunting, mysterious characters. Capricorns are the playful conjurers of the zodiac, and their mark on the literary world has been a formidable one.

THE CAPRICORN WRITER
A LITERARY HISTORY

Capricorn writers tend to have a gravitas to their work that is often the result either of their own tragic histories or of an ability to confront the tragic nature of reality with a clinical eye. In his Modernist triumph, *Cane*, Jean Toomer wrote unflinchingly about the Black experience. In his numerous poems and short stories, Edgar Allan Poe explored the darkest corners of the human psyche, and Zora Neale Hurston, in addition to being one of the most important novelists of the Harlem Renaissance, was a driven anthropologist who sought to study Vodou in Haiti. Meanwhile, Wilkie Collins, whose unconventional romantic life scandalized the masses, gave us what many consider the greatest detective novel of all time. Capricorn writers are powerful interpreters of reality, and they often spiral headfirst into the mystery that is the human experience. Wherever they are going, you will want to follow—if you dare.

CASE STUDY #1: JEAN TOOMER

It is a hallmark of the Capricorn to refuse definition, and nowhere is that more evident than in the life and work of Jean Toomer. One of the preeminent stylists of his time, he wrote only one successful book, *Cane* (1923)—a triumph of modernist technique that remains at the margins of literary history. An influential member of both the Harlem Renaissance and the Modernist movement, he identified fully with neither, instead choosing to forge his own path, one that would lead him through a cavalcade of alternative medicines, religions, and Eastern philosophy. Toomer was anything but a career writer. Instead, he was something perhaps more akin to a seeker.

Born to Nathan Toomer, a formerly enslaved man of mixed heritage, and his much younger, third wife, Nina Elizabeth Pinchback, a woman of color from a wealthy family, Jean Toomer's maternal grandfather, Pinckney Benton Stewart Pinchback, was the United States' first African American governor. After his father left and his parents divorced, Toomer's mother returned to her parents' home and raised Toomer under their influence. A sickly child, he suffered from a severe stomach ailment that once forced him to miss an entire year of school. This ill health would continue to haunt Toomer throughout his life and would lead him to investigate alternative therapies as an adult.

Extremely well educated, Toomer graduated from the prestigious M Street High School and went on to attend several colleges briefly, though he graduated from none. He maintained that they simply didn't have what he was looking for (and Capricorns often are very certain they know what they are looking for). Instead of completing a degree, Toomer moved to New York City and quickly became part of the literary community now known as the Harlem Renaissance. All it took was the publication of a few essays and a couple of short stories for the art world to recognize Toomer for the talent he was. His work was championed by

Waldo Frank (Libra), Sherwood Anderson (Virgo), and Hart Crane (Leo), and once he published his seminal work, *Cane*, his popularity exploded, earning him fans including literary giants Richard Wright (Virgo), Langston Hughes (Aquarius), and Nella Larsen (Aries, see page 22).

Cane remains a historically important work of art with a solidity to it that is a hallmark of the sign of Capricorn. Deeply mysterious, hauntingly beautiful, and decades, if not a full century, ahead of its time, *Cane* is composed of poetry, prose, and even a play script. It's an extremely early example of hybrid literature that seems at first glance to be so patchworked together that it can't possibly be coherent. And yet there is a glorious foundation to *Cane,* infused with lyric genius and thematic underpinnings that form a cohesive work that is at once an examination of racial injustice, feminine suffering, and pastoral beauty. Critics Charles Scruggs and Lee Van DeMarr see in it a Gothic detective story, one indebted to fellow Capricorn Edgar Allan Poe. Langston Hughes maintained it contained some of the finest prose ever written, and Toomer's own contemporary and close friend Waldo Frank called it, simply, "a mosaic." Moving seamlessly between forms and genres, *Cane* starts out with a bang:

KARINTHA

Her skin is like dusk on the eastern horizon
O cant you see it, O cant you see it,
Her skin is like dusk on the eastern horizon
. . . when the sun goes down.

Toomer goes on to describe a girl whose beauty draws unwanted male attention.

This interest of the male, who wishes to ripen a growing thing too soon, could mean no good to her . . . Karintha, at twelve, was a wild flash that told the other folks just what it was to live . . . Karintha's running was a whir. It had the sound of the red dust that sometimes makes a spiral in the road. At dusk, during the hush just after the sawmill had closed down, and before any of the women had started their supper-getting-ready songs, her voice, high-pitched, shrill, would put one's ears to itching. But no one thought to make her stop because of it. She stoned the cows, and beat her dog, and fought the other children.

Toomer's depiction of Karintha is immediate, alarming, and visceral, and the story he tells about and around her through a symphony of disparate voices—each adding a piece of the puzzle—is as beautiful as it is disconcerting. *Cane* is a work about identity as much as it is about shared history, but there is a focus on the body throughout—a subject that would preoccupy Toomer for much of his life. His frequent bouts of illness no doubt left him frustrated. In fact, mastery over the physical form was what first drew Toomer to fellow Capricorn George Gurdjieff, a Russian mystic who would greatly influence his life.

Gurdjieff taught that humans were cut off from attaining their rightful elevated spiritual state and, as a result, moved through life disconnected from their true selves. Through his multidisciplinary approach to spirituality, which he called "The Work," Gurdjieff believed that humans could reconnect with "objective consciousness," or wake up to the true nature of reality, which he termed "The Fourth Way."

Throughout his life, Toomer would search for spirituality or a higher state of being, moving through Gurdjieff's teachings to the Alexander Technique (an alternative medicine modality) to Dianetics to a long stint with the Quaker church, and finally returning to Gurdjieff. Along the way, Toomer often sought to discipline the body in an attempt to reconcile the corporeal self with the spiritual self. Much as Toomer resisted racial categorization (refusing to identify as either white or Black but as a "new race" or simply as an American), he also sought to reconcile the often painful nature of physical existence with the transcendent bliss of "objective consciousness."

Although spiritual seeking isn't an overtly Capricornian endeavor (on the surface, it would seem more Piscean in nature), the manner in which Toomer approached this spiritual enlightenment was intensely Capricorn. He didn't just try systems out; he threw himself into them, body and soul. After seeing a Gurd-

A portrait of Jean Toomer drawn in 1925 by Winold Reiss.

New York Public Library Digital Collections

jieff demonstration in New York, he was determined to study at the philosopher-mystic's institute in France, undertaking a grueling, physically and emotionally exhausting regimen that left him deeply transformed. When he returned to Harlem, he opened his own chapter of the institute, and of course he led it. His enthusiasm for "The Work" drew interest from literary luminaries and celebrities. Likewise, when he became a Quaker, he also became an advisor to college-aged members of the religion. His quest for spiritual succor led him into close contact with storied mystics, including the "Sleeping Prophet" himself, Edgar Cayce (Pisces).

By all accounts a fantastically handsome man, Jean Toomer married twice, first to Margery Latimer (Aquarius), who died in childbirth, and then to Marjorie Content (Aquarius), a gifted photographer. Toomer died in 1967.

CASE STUDY #2: EDGAR ALLAN POE

From the beginning, Edgar Allan Poe's life was fraught with tragedy. His father abandoned his mother, a famous actress, leaving her to raise three children alone. At the age of twenty-four, she succumbed to illness, dying when Poe was only two years old, possibly with him at her bedside witnessing her death. In the wake of her passing, he and his siblings were separated, with Poe being taken in by a foster family, John Allan and his wife, Frances. Although Frances Allan was kindly and doted on Poe, Mr. Allan seemed against him from the start, and this antipathy would continue for the entirety of their relationship, with the older man proving a constant source of rejection and pain for Poe. The heavy Capricorn influences of Saturn and Mars seemed determined to make themselves known in Poe's case.

While a teenager, Poe became a fan of the work of Lord Byron (Aquarius, see "A Note on Cusp Figures," page 274), and in his admiration, he took to dressing like the poet and writing his own maudlin verse. Already a melancholic boy, he seems to have been sent over the edge by the mental illness and subsequent death of a friend's mother to whom he had become close. He frequented her grave obsessively and is said to have kept a lock of her hair with him.

At age seventeen, Poe enrolled at the University of Virginia in Charlottesville. However, because Mr. Allan would concede to pay only a fraction of his tuition, Poe was consistently left struggling financially, often unable to pay for textbooks and other necessary items. In an effort to pay for school, Poe took up gambling but fell disastrously into debt. The situation was so bad that he was forced to drop out of school, and after a short stay in Boston, he enlisted in the army under a fake name to hide from his creditors.

Although responsibility and discipline aren't the first words that usually come to mind when one considers Poe, it seems that the army was a place that brought out his traditional Capricorn traits. He excelled in the military, ultimately attaining the rank of sergeant major, and with Mr. Allan's help, he gained entrance to West Point Academy. However, Poe's tenure at West Point was short-lived. Although an athletic young man, he found the drills grueling and the disciplinary approach excessively harsh. The responsible soldier of yore seemed to all but vanish. Instead, his rebellious nature came to the fore. In an obvious attempt to get kicked out, he stopped attending classes and was subsequently court-martialed and expelled from the academy.

When Poe was twenty, his foster mother, Mrs. Allan, died and he was once again heartbroken, losing yet another benevolent female figure to an early death. Deathly figures, women in particular, populate Poe's work. From the lost Lenore in "The Raven" (1845) to the titular character in "Ligeia" (1838), women in Poe's fictional world are often veritable wraiths of infirmity and decay. The loss of Poe's mother and foster mother no doubt served as inspirations for these depictions, but certainly the loss of his own young wife years later to tuberculosis played into this narrative tendency as well. And when we say young wife, we mean *young*. At age twenty-three, Poe married his thirteen-year-old cousin, Virginia Clemm (Leo).

There is great disagreement about the nature of this marriage. Was it normal for the time to marry one's first cousin? Maybe, but not *very*. But was it considered normal to marry a thirteen-year-old? Sort of, but not *really*. Their marriage was by all accounts a happy one, but there is some disagreement about whether or not the couple ever consummated the union. They were said to relate more like devoted siblings. Whatever the truth of the matter, Poe was absolutely devastated by her death.

Poe might not seem like a typical Capricorn. Driven as much by an impulse toward jocularity as by melancholy, he didn't adhere to rules and could hardly be considered responsible. Rather, he was almost driven to fly in the face of traditional society. An orphan and an unwanted foster child, Poe wore the mantle of the outcast from early on in his life. While at West Point, he entertained his fellow students with humorous poems often written at the expense of their professors, and he lived his life as something of a trickster. Instead of conforming to the stereotype of the determined leader that thrives on rules and regularity, his Capricornian personality can instead be seen in the deep melancholia evident in much of his work. To the casual observer, Capricorns' stoicism may be mistaken for unemotionality, but in reality, those emotions they keep so carefully hidden can be far deeper and more tortuous than those of even the most wounded Scorpio.

With his relentless focus on death and infirmity, on lost love and lost sanity, Poe poured his Capricorn heart onto the page and found himself in the darkest corners of the psyche. He has given us murderers who hide corpses behind walls and bury hearts beneath floorboards. He's thrilled us with entombed brides rising from graves and tormented Gothic bloodlines in moldering, crumbling manses, but behind it all is an incisive understanding of human emotion and, perhaps more importantly, grief.

Although the melancholy and the macabre may define the bulk of Poe's work, Capricorn's clarity of mind and penchant for calculation is often equally on display. His emphasis on cryptography in "The Gold-Bug" hints at the giddy ebullience of a schoolboy learning a new game, and indeed, it started something of a cryptography craze upon its publication. Likewise, his detailed explanation of ratiocination in "The Murders in the Rue Morgue" is the essence of Capricorn's love of structure and systematization. Poe's invention of the term (meaning careful analysis based on a combination of creative deduction and intellectual reasoning) and his in-text explanation of it would set up the preliminary rules of detective fiction for generations to come. Its echoes can clearly be heard in both Sherlock Holmes's deductive reasoning (Arthur Conan Doyle, Gemini, see page 64) and Hercule Poirot's process of stimulating "the little grey cells" (Agatha Christie, Virgo).

READING LIST:
Puzzle Books

1. A VOID by Georges Perec (Aries)

2. DUCKS, NEWBURYPORT by Lucy Ellmann (Libra)

3. HOUSE OF LEAVES by Mark Z. Danielewski (Aries)

4. CHOOSE YOUR OWN DISASTER by Dana Schwartz (Capricorn)

It's fitting that the man who gave us the first-ever detective story would die with an aura of intense mystery surrounding his demise. While on a speaking tour, and with long-term plans to reunite with his childhood sweetheart, Sarah Elmira Royster, Poe disappeared for several days. He was expected in New York, but instead turned up three days later in Baltimore, apparently drunk and wearing clothes that were not his own. He died shortly after. There are various theories about the circumstances surrounding his death, from kidnapping to alien abduction to meningitis, but for the end of his life to hold such mystery—for it to hew so closely to the plotlines of his stories—is, in the grand scheme of things, rather traditional. In that sense, he is the very picture of a conventional Capricorn.

CASE STUDY #3: ZORA NEALE HURSTON

If Poe can be seen as the outcast archetype of Capricorn, Zora Neale Hurston is much more of a traditionally Capricornian figure. Hurston grew up mostly in Eatonville, Florida, an entirely Black town of which her father was the mayor. Always a headstrong child, she and her father never saw eye to eye, and both agreed that Zora didn't quite fit in with the rest of the family. When her mother died when Hurston was thirteen, she was sent to boarding school in Jacksonville.

In some ways Hurston exemplifies some of the more classically conservative Capricorn traits. She was an academic who attended Howard University followed by Barnard, where she was the only African American student, followed by graduate school to study anthropology at Columbia University. While in graduate school, Hurston worked under the supervision of noted anthropologist Franz Boas (Cancer). Her field research focused heavily on southern folklore and traditions. As an anthropologist she courted controversy, and the authenticity of some of her work has been called into question in recent years, but there is no doubt that she was ambitious and that her aims and methods were groundbreaking in their own way. She was awarded a Guggenheim and in 1936 she traveled to Haiti, becoming the first Black female anthropologist to study the region. Prior to her visit, only white male anthropologists had done so. As a Black woman, Hurston felt she was inevitably doing deeper, more nuanced work, untarnished by racism, and she possessed an identity that she felt allowed her access to inner circles from which her predecessors had been barred. Her writing on the region is hypnotic, compelling, and nuanced, and Hurston was the first person to ever photograph someone who was believed to be a zombie.

Although she was famous during her day—and a major figure of the Harlem Renaissance—Hurston died on welfare and was buried in an unmarked grave. We owe her rediscovery to Alice Walker (Aquarius), who helped unearth her oeuvre in the 1970s and subsequently established her as part of the literary canon.

Hurston's literary achievements are vast and varied. She published short stories and novels; she wrote a play, *Mule Bone*, with Langston Hughes (Aquarius), and she published a memoir and a book that is at once an anthropological study and a travel memoir. Arguably her most famous work is the 1937 novel *Their Eyes Were Watching God*. Considered by many to be one of the best novels of all time, *Their Eyes Were Watching God* is now a mainstay of syllabi and considered a beloved classic, but it wasn't always the case. Although it published to critical success with white audiences, the novel was met with scorn by a great many of the Black literati, some of whom took issue with it not being "serious fiction." Ralph Ellison (Pisces) even denounced it as "calculated burlesque." Modern critics are more complimentary, with many seeing it as a groundbreaking novel in terms of its examination of female identity and sexual preference as well as for its folkloric influences.

Their Eyes Were Watching God, the story of a woman's struggle to find strength and independence in a world hell-bent on taking her agency, begins with typical Capricornian heaviness. Hurston writes:

> Ships at a distance have every man's wish on board.
> For some they come in with the tide. For others they
> sail forever on the horizon, never out of sight, never
> landing until the Watcher turns his eyes away in res-
> ignation, his dreams mocked to death by Time. That is
> the life of men.
>
> Now, women forget all those things they don't want to
> remember, and remember everything they don't want
> to forget. The dream is the truth. Then they act and do
> things accordingly.

But if the book begins with that burdened, tortured Capricornian spirit—that child forced to grow up too quickly—it ends with the kind of expansive hope that Capricorns are so good at conveying:

> She pulled in her horizon like a great fish-net.
> Pulled it from around the waist of the world and
> draped it over her shoulder. So much of life in its
> meshes! She called her soul to come and see.

CODA: WILKIE COLLINS

Wilkie Collins in some ways exemplifies both extremes of the Capricorn character. A social rebel who didn't believe in the institution of marriage, Collins had two romantic partners and two families, maintaining both openly for years. Although he had three children with Martha Rudd, he lived with Carolina Graves and raised her daughter as his own. This attack on one of the foundational aspects of society is emblematic of the black sheep side of Capricorn. And yet, Collins's writing was conventional in the sense that it established genre expectations that writers are still following to this day.

> We had our breakfasts—whatever happens in a house,
> robbery or murder, it doesn't matter, you must have your breakfast.
> —*THE MOONSTONE*

A good friend of Dickens's (Aquarius, see page 245), Collins started out writing short stories for Dickens's weekly magazines but soon transitioned to serialization. He rose to prominence with his serialized novel *The Woman in White* (1859), about a haunted woman and stolen identities. But it was his masterpiece, *The Moonstone* (1868), that would cement him as one of the most important figures of the mystery genre. Centered around a stolen necklace, *The Moonstone* was inspired by the real-life circumstances of the Constance Kent (Aquarius) case in which a teenage girl murdered her half-brother. The novel is remarkable for having established a number of conventions that have become staples of the genre, such as a murder located in a manor house and a twist ending. It was also the first mystery to introduce the concept of the red herring. Leave it to a Capricorn to defy conventions in his personal life only to end up creating new conventions in his professional life.

NOTES FOR WRITERS WITH OTHER CAPRICORN PLACEMENTS

WRITER'S CORNER

POSITIVE ASPECTS

When you set your mind to something, no one can stop you. Focus on a target and you are very likely to achieve your goals.

NEGATIVE ASPECTS

Not everyone is as responsible as you are. If you're part of a writing group, remember to try not to be overly domineering.

WRITER BEWARE

You can be prone to melancholy and self-doubt. Try to not second-guess yourself while drafting. Listen to your muse and simply allow yourself to create.

CAPRICORN MOON: You are a strong, practical writer who enjoys the process. You have no impulse to impress or imitate others. You have a fantastic sense of humor that you might let shine a bit more in your work. More than perhaps any other Moon sign, you have an ability to take constructive criticism with grace and equanimity. Would that we were all so fortunate!

CAPRICORN RISING: You often embody the most overt aspects of the sign in a way that is readily visible to others. You give off an air of patient determination that others admire. A born leader, you might consider putting yourself out there and organizing a series of local readings or even starting your own press.

MERCURY IN CAPRICORN: You are a detail-oriented dream of a person. You can take any sentence apart, diagram it, and reassemble it so it shines like a jewel, all while keeping your eye on the big-picture ideas of the larger piece. This gift, coupled with your ability to create veritable maps and spreadsheets in your head, makes you a phenomenal editor, both of your own work and that of others.

VENUS IN CAPRICORN: You have been endowed with a gift to write economical prose. You have a clear mind and an ability to convey your ideas in a cogent, straightforward manner. Chances are, you have never been accused of writing overly flowery or purple prose. You may want to explore your innate talent for essay writing.

MARS IN CAPRICORN: You have tremendous power and self-control. No obstacle is too great for you, and your endurance is second to none. You have it within you to write a truly formidable beast of a book. Leo Tolstoy, author of War and Peace, one of the longest novels ever written, had this placement. It's no joke.

TRY THIS!

+ TAKE a book you love and make a reverse outline of it. How did the author create this work? You can use your inherent understanding of structure to learn from the structures those you admire have already created.

+ TAKE a day and go play for a change. Be blithe and carefree. At the end of the day, just before bed, clear your mind and write a poem about your experience.

+ WRITE a ghost story. Take what haunts you and make it flesh and bone.

READER'S CORNER:

COMPATIBILITY CHART

Which Capricorn-composed book is most likely to appeal to you?
It depends on your sign. Look for your match below. And don't forget to
look at your rising and Moon signs if you know those.

SIGN	CLASSIC	MODERN
ARIES	J. R. R. TOLKIEN, *Lord of the Rings*	EDWIDGE DANTICAT, *Breath, Eyes, Memory*
TAURUS	ANNE BRONTË, *Agnes Grey*	C. D. WRIGHT, *The Other Hand*
GEMINI	MOLIÈRE, *Tartuffe, or, The Imposter*	WALTER MOSLEY, *Devil in a Blue Dress*
CANCER	JEAN RACINE, *Phèdre*	LAINI TAYLOR, *Strange the Dreamer*
LEO	ZORA NEALE HURSTON, *Their Eyes Were Watching God*	TANANARIVE DUE, *The Living Blood*
VIRGO	WILKIE COLLINS, *The Lady in White*	DAVID MITCHELL, *Cloud Atlas*

SIGN	CLASSIC	MODERN
LIBRA	E. M. FORSTER, *A Room with a View*	DAVID SEDARIS, *Naked*
SCORPIO	JEAN TOOMER, *Cane*	CHRIS ABANI, *The Secret History of Las Vegas*
SAGITTARIUS	A. A. MILNE, *Now We Are Six*	UMBERTO ECO, *Foucault's Pendulum*
CAPRICORN	EDGAR ALLAN POE, *Edgar Allan Poe: Collected Works*	WILLIAM GADDIS, *The Recognitions*
AQUARIUS	SIMONE DE BEAUVOIR, *She Came to Stay*	CLAUDIA RANKINE, *Citizen*
PISCES	ZORA NEALE HURSTON, *Tell My Horse*	HARUKI MURAKAMI, *The Wind-Up Bird Chronicle*

+ AQUARIUS +

AQUARIUS

THE VISIONARY WRITER

CURIOUSER AND CURIOUSER!

—Lewis Carroll

AQUARIUS 101

If there is a sign known for its cold, calculating brilliance, it's Aquarius. Ruled by the element air, Aquarius lives the life of the mind. But while its fellow air signs (Gemini and Libra) may be buoyed along by similar brainy energies, Aquarius shares none of their playfulness. A fixed sign originally governed by the planet Saturn (the planet of conservative discipline), Aquarius is the sign of the hermit. An Aquarius can be set in their ways and are often found living on the outskirts of society where they actively disrupt convention. The paradox is that if there is a sign that is *about* society, it's Aquarius. Being about society, though, doesn't mean being about people's feelings. An Aquarius is a humanitarian, but far from a saint. However, unlike with Scorpio (the most unfairly maligned sign), there's never anything personal about an Aquarius's attack. They don't mean to hurt you. They just literally don't care. They care about social justice. They care about equality. They can envision a utopian society better than any other sign and want to work to create it. They just don't care too much about you—except insofar as you are a part of society. And in that sense, they love you more than anything in the world.

Fellow air signs might privilege freedom above all else, but they tend to focus on personal freedom (Libra's freedom to love indiscriminately and Gemini's freedom to talk indiscriminately), while the sense of freedom that appeals to Aquarius is the universal kind. Every single living creature

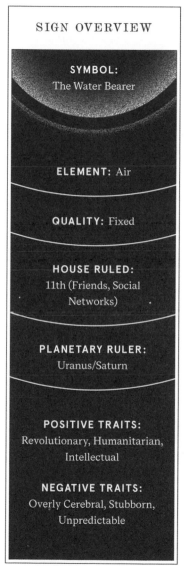

SIGN OVERVIEW

SYMBOL:
The Water Bearer

ELEMENT: Air

QUALITY: Fixed

HOUSE RULED:
11th (Friends, Social
Networks)

PLANETARY RULER:
Uranus/Saturn

POSITIVE TRAITS:
Revolutionary, Humanitarian,
Intellectual

NEGATIVE TRAITS:
Overly Cerebral, Stubborn,
Unpredictable

matters to the Aquarius. The tricky part is that they mostly matter in the collective. They don't so much matter individually. If Aquarius sounds like a mass of contradictions, this is due in part to the fact that the sign is ruled by two planets that are polar opposites in nature: Saturn, the Great Malefic, and Uranus, the planet of surprise.

Uranus was discovered by accident in 1781 and subsequently assigned as Aquarius's modern ruler. As home to the sign of eccentricity, innovation, and even genius, Uranus is the planet of newness and progress. Conversely, Aquarius's ancient ruler, Saturn, is the planet of restriction, discipline, and—if we're not careful—destruction. When these competing forces clash, they create tsunamis of chaos and unrest. That essential collision is at the heart of every Aquarius. They want the new but they are governed by the old. They want progress but can be ruthlessly conservative about how they accomplish it. They are walking contradictions—relatable yet unknowable, humanitarian yet at times robotic. But whatever you make of them, they are never to be trifled with.

Despite Saturn's dominating nature, it is perhaps Uranus that gives us the deepest insight into the nature of the Aquarius. The discovery of Uranus, that planet of shock and surprise, of sea changes and societal disruptions, coincided with the Age of Enlightenment. A time of revolution and intellectual flourishing, it was also when the academy turned its back on astrology. Once considered a science respected by intellectuals like Aristotle and Hippocrates, astrology was unceremoniously banished from the realm of the intellectual elite by the Scientific Revolution. One could (very unscientifically) argue that Uranus's discovery brought about the delegitimization of astrology itself. Humankind was at a turning point during which it shifted its gaze away from the stars and toward the laboratory, test tube, and microscope. In the interest of the greater good, Uranus showed up with a shock and destroyed the very discipline that supplied its own authority. This kind of brutal yet ethical practicality is Aquarius in a nutshell.

THE AQUARIUS WRITER
A LITERARY HISTORY

Aquarius writers often have a cause, though sometimes that cause is inscrutable, transitory, or simply too far above the rest of our heads to be understood. Anne Spencer mixed art with humanitarianism, Dickens campaigned for the poor, Lewis Carroll (perhaps inadvertently) wrote a feminist classic, and Frederick Douglass's abolitionist philosophy changed the shape of society forever. Aquarius writers challenge norms, break molds, and approach absolutely everything with a decidedly iconoclastic and emotionally detached execution that often verges on genius.

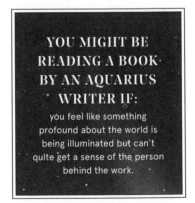

YOU MIGHT BE READING A BOOK BY AN AQUARIUS WRITER IF:
you feel like something profound about the world is being illuminated but can't quite get a sense of the person behind the work.

CASE STUDY #1: FREDERICK DOUGLASS

Frederick Douglass was a prominent abolitionist, social reformer, writer, orator, and statesman. He believed that oratory and education were routes to freedom and developed these passions all his life. While enslaved as a child, Douglass listened carefully to older generations discuss their experiences of the Middle Passage and then bore witness to these narratives as a public figure.

Douglass found a way to get his hands on a copy of *The Columbian Orator*, an anthology of excerpts from radical thinkers including Socrates and Cicero, which he memorized and which ultimately helped him gain literacy. He held a Sunday school class at which he taught other enslaved people to read and proclaimed that he knew that learning constituted "the pathway from slavery to freedom." Despite the common misconception that Frederick Douglass's key influences were the white abolitionists with whom he joined in arms, he maintained that fellow enslaved men taught him to debate, reason, and understand what freedom meant.

Douglass's oratory was so powerful, it caused his opponents to doubt that he was telling the truth. This talent inspired his supporters across the Atlantic to pay off his owner so that, having fled the country, Douglass could return to the United States a free man. While Douglass depended on the spoken word to push past dominant cultural narratives and communicate freedom, he also rewrote the American story from his perspective in three great autobiographical works: *A Narrative of the Life of Frederick Douglass, an American Slave* (1845); *My Bondage and My Freedom* (1855); and *Life and Times of Frederick Douglass* (1881, revised 1892). Pushing back against the dominant white abolitionist belief that freed slaves should settle in a colony outside the United States, Douglass stood up to figures including Abraham Lincoln (also an Aquarius) to proclaim: "We were born here and here we will remain."

What can we make of Frederick Douglass's birth, and what can it tell us about the futurity encoded in radical, Aquarian literature?

Born into slavery in 1818, Frederick Douglass never knew his exact birthday. However, later in life he chose to celebrate his birthday on February 14, remembering that his mother, Harriet Bailey, from whom he was separated in infancy, called him her "Little Valentine."

While Douglass hardly knew his mother, she was a great source of inspiration to him. She had learned to read, had a gift with language, and poured love into him in the very limited opportunities she had. Douglass remembered her comforting him at night: "I do not recollect of ever seeing my mother by the light of day. She was with me in the night. She would lie down with me, and get me to sleep, but long before I waked she was gone." Douglass's fight for freedom and justice was fueled, in part, by two guiding motifs connected to this attachment to and loss of his mother: that of the slave mother who has many children but no family and that of the Black woman resisting by any means necessary.

Our Sun sign connects us to the day of our birth, to the light and illumination that shines on our mother's laboring body, whether the Sun floods the fields outside a hut or reflects and refracts off the Moon, whether we feel the warmth of the Sun's light or only feel its presence in the darkness. Frederick Douglass's mother, Harriet Bailey, may have known the exact date of his birth on the Gregorian calendar, hence her sweet nickname for her baby, or she may not have known for sure. Could she know he would learn to read and write and gain his freedom? Could she feel how he would fight to reshape the nation? Could she intuit how desperately we would still need his example today?

Futurity is a project shared by the mother and the writer, and by claiming February 14 as the day Harriet labored, Douglass also lay claim to his Aquarian nature.

Douglass is far from the only Aquarius writer to use his literary gifts to imagine and shape Black futurity. Langston Hughes, one of the great

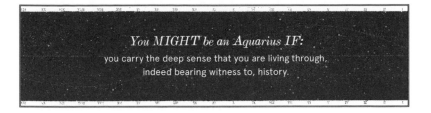

You MIGHT be an Aquarius IF:
you carry the deep sense that you are living through,
indeed bearing witness to, history.

poets of the Harlem Renaissance, is another shining example. In his poem "Mother to Son," Hughes imagines a mother encouraging her son by recounting her own trials and tribulations: "Don't you fall now—/ For I'se still goin', honey." In these lines we find echoes of Hughes's grandmother's profound influence on his sense of pride and purpose, and if we keep them in mind as we look at the history of powerful Aquarian writing about Black futures, we might also catch whispers of Frederick Douglass's mother comforting him at night, an act of love that encouraged him to keep climbing toward freedom.

What did Frederick Douglass do with his freedom? He used it to free others. Toni Morrison (also an Aquarius) writes that the "function of freedom is to free someone else." This revolutionary ethos speaks to the potential of the Aquarius writer to radically alter their historical moment. Audre Lorde, the self-described "Black, lesbian, mother, warrior, poet" who shared Toni Morrison's February birthday, famously wrote that "silence will not protect you," and dedicated her voice to the protection of others.

The Aquarius writer may have a deep sense that they are not of their time, but instead belong to the past and future simultaneously. As Frederick Douglass and others have shown, an Aquarius possesses the potential to unite past and future in their work, to bear witness to historical sufferings while moving the world toward greater liberation.

READING LIST:

Scandalous Novels

1. THE MONK by Matthew "Monk" Lewis (Cancer)

2. MATHILDA by Mary Shelley (Virgo)

3. THE AWAKENING by Kate Chopin (Aquarius)

4. LADY CHATTERLEY'S LOVER by D. H. Lawrence (Virgo)

5. LOLITA by Vladimir Nabokov (Taurus)

CASE STUDY #2: LEWIS CARROLL

If there are those who epitomize the positive aspects of Aquarius (Douglass), and those who epitomize the negative aspects of the sign (cough, Byron, see "A Note on Cusp Figures," page 274), there are also some who remain inscrutably uncategorized between the two polarities. And it is here that we arrive at Lewis Carroll. Was he a genius who revolutionized children's literature and, in giving us the first female lead in the genre, a pioneer of gender equality? Or was he a repressed (or possibly even unrepressed) pedophile who fetishized the children for whom his stories were written? Could he have been both?

When discussing Carroll's biography, it's difficult not to address the unsettling mystery surrounding his relationship with Alice Liddell (Taurus), the child who inspired the lead character of his Alice novels. A one-sentence summary of that relationship might look like this: creepy Oxford don dotes on the dean's daughter and writes a book about her before the family decides he's become overly affectionate in his attentions and cuts off the relationship. Conversely, it might look like this: young math professor babysits little girls and, at their insistence, tells them a story, which one of them—Alice—compels him to write down, before having a break with the family that might have nothing to do with Alice at all. Or it could even look like this: creepy Oxford don has inappropriate relationship with Alice's *older sister*, who is above the age of consent (but the age of consent was twelve, so . . .). The question of his intent is further confused by the fact that after his relationship with the Liddells, he continued to bestow affection on young girls. Or was it on teenage girls and young women? Did an early biographer try to make his attention to young, unmarried women seem less scandalous by lying about their ages and making them seem to be children, inadvertently making Carroll sound like a card-carrying pedophile?

A portrait of Alice Liddell, circa 1860, photograph by Lewis Carroll.

If you want to stop reading now, we don't blame you. Sometimes an Aquarius makes you want to stop reading. So let us turn for a moment to some of his Aquarian biographical elements. Lewis Carroll's real name was Charles Lutwidge Dodgson. He was the son of a clergyman and the oldest of eleven children. Carroll spent his youth entertaining his younger siblings, telling them stories and inventing games for them to play. A gifted mathematician, he went on to study at Oxford before eventually becoming a mathematics lecturer and don. It was at Oxford, when Carroll was twenty-four, that he met young Alice Liddell and her sisters, Lorina and Edith. The girls were the daughters of the dean of the college, and Carroll initially asked them to sit for photographs for him. Aquarius is the sign of innovation and technology, so it's not surprising that Carroll was one of the early adopters of photography as an art form.

An Aquarian hallmark of Carroll's work is a sense of shifting perceptions of reality, a celebration of logic games and puzzles. Famously, the story of *Alice's Adventures in Wonderland* (1865) was birthed one day during a boat trip with the Liddell girls, but along for that ride was a colleague and fellow math professor, Robinson Duckworth. That Carroll was telling a story to entertain both children and a math professor simultaneously is evident in the work and is perhaps even the reason for its longevity and mass appeal. The riddles he creates are actually riddles, and his logic puzzles really can puzzle. There is a sense that the laws of neither physics nor polite society apply to his fictional worlds.

YOU MIGHT BE AN AQUARIUS IF: you have unpopular favorites. As a kid, you clamored for Almond Joy while trick-or-treating. Table tennis is your sport of choice. At the zoo, you linger by the vulture exhibit. You can't help it—you just love to root for an underdog.

"Please come back, and finish your story!" Alice called after it.
And the others all joined in chorus, "Yes, please do!" But the Mouse only shook its head impatiently, and walked a little quicker.

—ALICE'S ADVENTURES IN WONDERLAND

Carroll possessed a meticulous attention to detail that shows itself in the precision of his craftsmanship and in his intricate drawings. In the original handwritten manuscript he gave to Alice Liddell, there isn't a single misspelling, nor a single word crossed out. The drawings are exquisite, and the penmanship is neat and precise. In this manuscript, we observe the Aquarian penchant for fastidiousness and attention to detail.

Alice's Adventures in Wonderland and its sequel, *Through the Looking-Glass* (1871), remain some of the most popular works of literature ever composed. The original book has never been out of print, has been translated into more than a hundred languages, and has been adapted into numerous films. Perhaps without intending to, Carroll created the

An original manuscript page from *Alice's Adventures Under Ground*, featuring an illustration by Lewis Carroll.

The British Library

quintessential work of enduring children's literature, all while breaking multiple conventions and challenging the mores of the time.

Although Lewis himself may have been a quiet academic, his more rebellious Aquarian traits come out in his depiction of Alice. She is brave, wise, self-possessed, and a character who meets every challenge head-on and refuses to be duped. When she falls down that rabbit hole and finds herself in Wonderland, she isn't afraid, merely curious. She doesn't shy away from drinking the potion that will eventually allow her to enter the next realm. She is a classic Aquarius, open to adventure and delaying judgment until she has a complete understanding of the facts. She is also an egalitarian, as likely to take advice from a bodiless cat as to try to speak to a mouse in its native French, though her understanding of the language might leave something to be desired. Sometimes an Aquarius thinks they know more than they do, and that, coupled with their stubbornness, can get them into a spot of trouble now and then.

Once in Wonderland, Alice observes with detached Aquarian distaste the injustice of the Queen of Hearts and the general chaos of the land. She'll try to play croquet with a flamingo if that's what the locals do, but she isn't going to be surprised when it doesn't work. She questions and challenges everything and everyone, never accepting a simple answer and never allowing herself to be patronized or talked down to.

There is a paradoxical feel to Carroll's artistic intentions. The creation of this heroine seems subversive, feminist even, and yet Carroll was politically and socially conservative. Similarly, he pokes fun at the religious dogmatism typical in children's literature but was himself an ordained minister. To an Aquarius, though, these contradictions are less contradictions and more a reflection of a sense of realism. The Aquarius doesn't accept anyone's rules and morals except for their own, and in contrast to fellow rule breakers like Aries and Sagittarius, Aquarius is rather strict about abiding by the rules they create. But they simply must be their *own* rules, never society's.

Although he wrote under a pseudonym and wished to maintain as much anonymity as he could, Carroll's fame erupted after the publication of *Alice's Adventures in Wonderland*, and he continued to write throughout his life. In addition to writing and photography, Carroll excelled as a mathematician, publishing eleven books on subjects ranging from geometry to algebra to mathematical logic, and he continued to teach at Oxford. He died in 1898 of pneumonia after catching the flu.

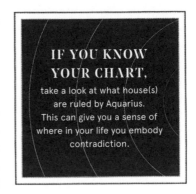

IF YOU KNOW YOUR CHART, take a look at what house(s) are ruled by Aquarius. This can give you a sense of where in your life you embody contradiction.

CASE STUDY #3: ANNE SPENCER

Sometimes an Aquarius lives their life as a form of artistic practice, and it is only through the intervention of others that their work reaches a wider audience. Such is the case with Anne Spencer, who despite never living in Harlem became a central figure of the Harlem Renaissance, and who despite publishing only thirty poems in her lifetime became the first African American woman to be published in *The Norton Anthology of Modern Poetry.*

Born in Danville, Virginia, in 1882, Spencer was the daughter of parents whose views on raising a child were wildly divergent. Her parents, who had been born into

Anne Spencer's garden studio; photograph by James Camp.

slavery, eventually split, with Anne and her mother moving to West Virginia. Despite the distance, Anne's father stayed very involved in parenting Anne, and was insistent that she receive the best education possible. Anne was an exceedingly bright child, and her father was always proud to show off her intelligence, but he knew that innate intelligence also requires proper nurturing. When she was eleven, he insisted that she attend the prestigious Virginia Theological Seminary and College in Lynchburg. This decision turned out to be a good one, because Anne excelled at school, distinguishing herself in literature and languages in particular. It was at the seminary that she would eventually meet a handsome young man named Edward Spencer (Taurus) who was gifted in math and science. The two fell in love and began tutoring each other in their respective specialties.

After graduating as the valedictorian in 1899, Anne went on to marry Ed, and the two set up a gorgeous home in Lynchburg, where Ed became an entrepreneur and the first Black mail carrier in the city. Anne set her artistic talents to creating an ethereally beautiful garden at their home, filled with winding walkways, a lily pond, and whimsical birdhouses. Ed built her a work studio in the garden, which they named Edankraal, a name created by combining both of their names with *kraal*, a South African word meaning "enclosure."

The couple raised two daughters, Bethel Calloway and Alroy Sarah, as well as a son, Chauncey Edward (Scorpio), who would go on to become a pilot and who proved instrumental in the organization of the Tuskegee Airmen. Very active in the civil rights movement, Anne and Ed Spencer helped to establish the local chapter of the NAACP. They also hosted Black travelers who, because of their race, were refused service at local inns. The result was the creation of a flourishing artistic and intellectual center at the Spencers' elegant Queen Anne–style home, with such luminaries as W. E. B. Du Bois (Pisces, see page 260), Marian Anderson (Pisces), and Langston Hughes (Aquarius) passing through. It was in the midst of one such visit that James Weldon Johnson (Gemini) discovered some of Anne's poetry, and the rest is history.

Anne Spencer's life was the apotheosis of an Aquarian existence. Aquarius governs the 11th House of friends and social circles, and it is the sign of the staunch humanitarian, so it is no wonder that she drew so many intellectuals to her. Along with her Taurus partner, who no doubt helped create a stable sense of place, she was able to fashion a home away from home for the Harlem Renaissance and its artists. She did all this while also devoting herself to humanitarian causes. But an Aquarius also needs a touch of the mystical in their life, and it was her devotion to her garden and her extraordinary poetic gifts that brought her this enchantment. Laden with mythical imagery and composed mostly in classical forms, Spencer's poems celebrate the natural world, conjuring up other times and other realities, distinguishing themselves as lustrously Aquarian.

In her professional life, Spencer was a librarian and an educator. Notably, she vastly expanded the collection at Paul Laurence Dunbar High School. At home she often spent time inside Edankraal, which, in addition to being an artist's studio, functioned as a library and archive. She spent most of her time, though, in her famous garden, tending to it with the same precision and delicacy she bestowed upon her poems. It was in that garden that she composed most of her work, often drawing on her immediate surroundings for inspiration and imagery, and then infusing her lush language with mythic themes. Sitting out among the laurel and phlox, or perhaps beside her lily pond that was adorned with a sculpture given to the Spencers by W. E. B. Du Bois, Anne Spencer wrote of far-reaching Aquarian visions as in her poem "Questing":

> Let me learn now where Beauty is;
> My day is spent too far toward night
> To wander aimlessly and miss her place
> To grope, eyes shut, and fingers touching space.

Her poetry is transcendent, but it is something she said in passing that perhaps best sums up her Aquarian penchant for mixing art and life. When biographer Dr. Johnny Lee Greene once asked why she never wrote a novel, she replied simply, "I've been too busy living one."

Anne Spencer died in 1975, eleven years after her beloved partner.

CODA: CHARLES DICKENS

Charles Dickens's life was, well . . . it was Dickensian. The fact that we have a word for that shows you how much of an Aquarius he was. Born in 1812, Dickens was one of eight children. His family fell on hard times, and at the age of twelve Dickens was forced to withdraw from school and work long days in a blacking factory. The conditions were abominable and the injustice of his situation was not lost on him, even at that young age. This almost preternatural ability to identify injustice is one of the most admirable Aquarian traits, second only to the determination to pull that injustice out at the roots and destroy it.

Without much formal education, Dickens found fame by his mid-twenties, probably due in part to his very Aquarian ability to be at the forefront of trends and social transformation. Indeed, his devotion to social justice never flagged, and he continued to address issues of inequality in his work (perhaps most seriously in *David Copperfield*) as well as to lecture against the horrors of slavery in the United States. He also supported women writers, publishing many in the weekly magazines he edited, *Household Words* and *All Year Round*. His innovative reinvention of the serialized novel helped to popularize fiction and make it more accessible. Along with several of his best-known novels (*A Tale of Two Cities, Great Expectations*), his magazines also serialized works by writers like Elizabeth Gaskell (Libra), Wilkie Collins (Capricorn, see page 225), and Amelia Edwards (Gemini, see page 68).

The injustice of class structures and the plight of the poor were central themes in Dickens's work. His first novel, *Oliver Twist* (1837), tells the story of a street urchin forced to live by his wits in a society that has neither sympathy for nor interest in the poor, especially poor children. *A Tale of Two Cities* (1859) further focuses on this inequality, and indeed one would be hard-pressed to find a work of Dickens's that doesn't in some way touch upon justice, reform, inequality, or poverty. *Great Expectations* (1861) highlights the disparity between the circumstances of the wealthy and the poor, examining greed and the fixed nature of social structures. In *David Copperfield* (1849–1850), his most autobiographical novel, Dickens is also formally innovative, portraying a character's daily life from childhood well into adulthood. But it is *A Christmas Carol* (1843) that had perhaps the largest impact in terms of social change. The story of a greedy man forced to reckon with his wicked ways, *A Christmas Carol* tugged the heartstrings by showing the hardship of an impoverished family at Christmas. It was an enormous financial and critical success, allowing Dickens to tour the world to sold-out concert halls. Moreover, it brought about real progress, with some business owners reporting that they changed the way they treated employees after being emotionally moved by the plight of Tiny Tim's family. When people argue that social change can't come from fiction, it's important to remember that it can and it has.

NOTES FOR WRITERS WITH OTHER AQUARIUS PLACEMENTS

WRITER'S CORNER

POSITIVE ASPECTS

Your writing is on the right side of history, at once revolutionary, humanitarian, and intellectual.

NEGATIVE ASPECTS

You can spiral into overthinking or refuse to shift your own expectations to follow the work.

WRITER BEWARE

Satire comes easily to you, which is a great thing for your writing but might strain your relationships with collaborators.

AQUARIUS MOON: If your Moon is in Aquarius, much of this will likely resonate with you on an emotional level. Especially as children, a lunar Aquarius can feel like they just don't fit in. Writing a memoir that examines those difficult childhood emotions might do wonders for you and help you connect with readers who have dealt with similar issues. Or why not try your hand at writing for children? Tap into some of those emotions and memories and use them as a bridge to communicate with a younger generation.

AQUARIUS RISING: You often physically embody the most eccentric aspects of the sign in a way that is readily visible to others. People might think you're aloof or intimidating. As such, maybe you want to think about using the awe-inspiring effect you have on others for the greater good. Give revolutionary speeches, organize counterculture artist events, head up a literary salon. People will be drawn to your light like lit-loving moths.

MERCURY IN AQUARIUS: You have a knack for clarity and a flair for the technical. The trick is making sure that your visionary ideas aren't too general. Remember, the best way to appeal to a general audience is through the specific.

VENUS IN AQUARIUS: You often locate a great deal of importance and emotion in your friendships and social groups. If this is the case, why not try your hand at a novel about friendship? It's not often that friendship stories are prioritized in our society. You might be just the writer to change that.

MARS IN AQUARIUS: You embody the passionate, humanitarian zeal of the sign, so why not get out there and tell the world what you really think? You're capable of revolutionary visions, so write a manifesto or dig deep into the ancient art of rhetoric. You have the ability to change the world. A pretty big order, we know. But we also know you're up to it.

TRY THIS!

+ THINK of a question that feels forbidden. This can be personal to you, something you shouldn't bring up at a dinner party, or anything in between. Write down the question and then the first five responses that come to mind. Pick one of those responses, ask a follow-up question, and repeat the exercise.

+ THINK of something about you that might surprise others. This could be a recurring thought or dream, a private interest, or something that happened to you in the past. Now, confess this surprising fact about yourself in the form of a flash fiction story.

+ THINK of an issue that is important to you. What would someone need to understand in order to see the issue the way you do? Write a work of fiction that provides the reader with the keys to understanding.

READER'S CORNER:

COMPATIBILITY CHART

Which Aquarius-composed book is most likely to appeal to you?
It depends on your sign. Look for your match below. And don't forget to
look at your rising and Moon signs if you know those.

SIGN	CLASSIC	MODERN
ARIES	KATE CHOPIN, *The Awakening*	TONI MORRISON, *Beloved*
TAURUS	ANTON CHEKHOV, *The Collected Works of Anton Chekhov*	GERTRUDE STEIN, *Tender Buttons*
GEMINI	LEWIS CARROLL, *Sylvie and Bruno, Sylvie and Bruno Concluded*	FRANK MILLER, *Daredevil*
CANCER	CHARLES DICKENS, *David Copperfield*	AMY TAN, *The Joy Luck Club*
LEO	CHARLES DICKENS, *Great Expectations*	VIRGINIA WOOLF, *To the Lighthouse*
VIRGO	EDITH WHARTON, *The House of Mirth*	LANGSTON HUGHES, *The Collected Poems of Langston Hughes*

SIGN	CLASSIC	MODERN
LIBRA	E. T. A HOFFMANN, *The Sandman*	PAUL AUSTER, *The New York Trilogy*
SCORPIO	LORD BYRON, *Don Juan*	WILLIAM S. BURROUGHS, *Naked Lunch*
SAGITTARIUS	JULES VERNE, *Twenty Thousand Leagues Under the Sea*	JACK SPICER, *The Collected Books of Jack Spicer*
CAPRICORN	EDITH WHARTON, *The Age of Innocence*	ALICE WALKER, *The Color Purple*
AQUARIUS	FREDERICK DOUGLASS, *Narrative of the Life of Frederick Douglass, an American Slave*	JAMES JOYCE, *Ulysses*
PISCES	ANTON CHEKHOV, *The Cherry Orchard*	JACQUELINE WOODSON, *Brown Girl Dreaming*

✦ PISCES ✦

PISCES

THE WRITER CAUGHT BETWEEN WORLDS

BENEATH THE VEIL LAY RIGHT AND WRONG, VENGEANCE
AND LOVE, AND SOMETIMES THROWING ASIDE THE VEIL,
A SOUL OF SWEET BEAUTY AND TRUTH STOOD REVEALED.

—W. E. B. Du Bois

PISCES 101

Pisces bear the mantle of the hopeless romantics of the zodiac. And while the old adage may be true that they fall in love easily and often, they also have something of a wandering spirit about them. They may be the first to show up at a doorstep, heart clutched and flowers in hand, but they are just as apt to wander off the next day to chase after butterflies . . . or an equally enthralling mate. This is in part due to their status as a mutable water sign (their feelings are intense, but they are also changeable) and the fact that Venus is exalted, or especially potent, in their sign. Indeed, the goddess of beauty informs almost everything they do, making them drawn to and gifted at artistic expression perhaps more than any other sign. Their inherent mutability and artistic temperament also make them incredibly fun to be around. In fact, they are almost always up for an adventure, but because they are such quiet artists, you may forget to invite them along.

Pisces rules the 12th House of the zodiac—the house of the unconscious. As such, they are often tapped in to the subtler aspects of existence in a way that might elude a more grounded sign. As the sign of the mystic, they are often drawn to spirituality—whether that takes the form of traditional religion or whether it falls along the lines of an interest in the paranormal. They have a deep knowing that there is more to reality than can be perceived by the naked eye. Pisces is the sign of the psychic, but one

SIGN OVERVIEW

SYMBOL:
The Fish

ELEMENT: Water

QUALITY: Mutable

HOUSE RULED:
12th (The Unknown)

PLANETARY RULER:
Neptune/Jupiter

POSITIVE TRAITS:
Spiritual, Kindhearted,
Artistic

NEGATIVE TRAITS:
Delusional, Escapist,
Self-Righteous

needn't believe in crystals and mediums to believe that Pisces are able to see things that others miss. They tend to be deeply empathetic, immediately tapping into how others feel without any need for verbal expression. Whether they are seeing beyond the veil, reading energy, or simply processing subtle information that might remain in the realm of the unconscious for a different sign, Pisces can read a room like no other.

A double-bodied sign, Pisces is also blessed with a double planetary rulership. Their modern ruler is Neptune, all watery emotional depth and otherworldly dreaminess, but their ancient ruler is Jupiter, who endows the sign with a quietly larger-than-life aura and a deep sense of their own greatness. That self-assuredness may be overlaid with varying degrees of shyness and insecurity, but at their core, Pisces have a solidity and strength to them that is often overlooked. It's easy to underestimate a Pisces, but never for very long.

Doubleness is at the very center of the Piscean nature and is reflected in their symbol of the fish, for if you look closely, Pisces isn't just a pair of fish, but a pair of fish swimming in opposite directions, creating a circle of constant tension and change. Just as one aspect of a Pisces may break through the surface, shining forth for all to see, another dives deep into the midnight zone where their true self remains hidden, even to their closest allies. These fishy creatures may be enchanting, but they are ultimately unknowable. And that's just how they like it.

THE PISCES WRITER:
A LITERARY HISTORY

Pisces writers challenge us in ways we may never think to challenge ourselves. E. Pauline Johnson made us question the space between reality and performance. W. E. B. Du Bois used his voice to fight for equality. Zitkála-Šá showed that sometimes the best path for a Pisces is all paths, and Arthur Machen used his Piscean mysticism to seek beyond the confines of this reality.

CASE STUDY #1: E. PAULINE JOHNSON (TEKAHIONWAKE)

E. Pauline Johnson (who also went by the name Tekahionwake) was a member of the Six Nations, born in Ontario to Emily Howells, a British woman, and John Smoke Johnson (Sagittarius), the son of famed Mohawk chief George Henry Martin Johnson (Libra). Educated mostly at home and speaking both English and Mohawk in the house, Johnson read widely, influenced by her mother's literary background, and learned storytelling tradition from her father and grandfather.

Johnson began writing and performing her work after her father's death left her mother in financial difficulty. Pisces's doubling nature is writ large in Johnson. She was an expert at existing in a space of doubleness, and indeed the name she chose for herself can be interpreted as "double life." Not only did she fully embrace and embody both of her

Johnson, E. Pauline.

A portrait of E. Pauline Johnson, also known as Tekahionwake.

New York Public Library Digital Collections

cultural identities, she actively performed both, often splitting the staged recitations of her work into two acts. In the first part of her performance, she dressed as a "traditional Indian," only to reappear onstage after intermission dressed as a stereotypical Englishwoman. In fact, the dress she wore for that initial act was in no way traditional Mohawk but was rather an aggregation of Indian-esque paraphernalia, mostly purchased, that she combined to create the spectacle of Native culture. And indeed, she was a Canadian woman, not English as her mother had been. Even her Englishness was a kind of exaggerated performance. The collective result was captivating, and she was incredibly popular during her time. In fact, she earned a call for an encore during her very first performance, a literary event at which she was the only woman in attendance.

Although the surface of her performance may have been a kind of artifice, the foundations of her work and the ideas expressed therein were grounded in an authenticity that was rarely seen at the time. Johnson wrote about passion and sexuality at a time when few women dared to do so. She also addressed racism head-on. Her stories often involved the collision of white and Native value systems, and she expertly unpacked the hypocrisy of white European colonizers imposing their own beliefs on people without a modicum of genuine cultural exchange. This is apparent in her story "As It Was in the Beginning," in which a young married woman of mixed heritage is told by her white husband that she has brought shame on them by being honest when asked about her parents' marriage (they were wed according to traditional Native customs instead of by missionaries).

Balking at the suggestion that she should feel shame, she addresses the elephant in the room directly, pointing out that despite living among her people and supposedly being one of the "good" white people, he still harbors prejudice and clearly thinks his ancestral ways are superior to hers. The main character, Christie, tells him she doesn't need the law to verify a marriage commitment:

> Law? My people have no priest, and my nation cringes not to law. Our priest is purity, and our law is honour. Priest? Was there a priest at the most holy marriage known to humanity—that stainless marriage whose offspring is the God you white men told my pagan mother of?

She then turns the tables, explaining that if he doesn't recognize her people's marriage contracts, then she doesn't recognize his and therefore they are not married. When he protests, she doubles down.

> "I tell you we are not married. Why should I recognize the rites of your nation when you do not acknowledge the rites of mine? According to your own words, my parents should have gone through your church ceremony as well as through an Indian contract; according to *my* words, *we* should go through an Indian contract as well as through a church marriage. If their union is illegal, so is ours. If you think my father is living in dishonour with my mother, my people will think I am living in dishonour with you. How do I know when another nation will come and conquer you as you white men conquered us? And they will have another marriage rite to perform, and they will tell us another

truth, that you are not my husband, that you are but disgrac-
ing and dishonouring me, that you are keeping me here, not as
your wife, but as your—your *squaw.*" The terrible word had never
passed her lips before, and the blood stained her face to her very
temples. She snatched off her wedding ring and tossed it across
the room, saying scornfully, "That thing is as empty to me as the
Indian rites to you."

The passage is cutting and direct, but Johnson's style remains lyrical, almost dreamlike—until Christie uses a misogynistic and racist slur,
breaking through the glamour of the prose and calling out bigotry for the
utter horror that it is. Pisces are capable of living dreamily in the ether,
but when they want to speak the truth, they do so bluntly and with the
force of an unflinching prophet.

A great beauty (Pisces are often easy on the eyes), Johnson was
inundated with suitors and was said to have refused multiple marriage
proposals in her life. She remained single and childless, claiming her
platonic friendships with women as her dearest relationships. As biographers Veronica Strong-Boag and Carole Gerson write:

Ultimately, for all her romantic attachments, Johnson was nur-
tured through her life by a strong network of female friends who
made their lives outside of the Native community. Their importance is best attested in her own words: "women are fonder of me
than men are. I have had none fail me, and I hope I have failed
none. It is a keen pleasure for me to meet a congenial woman, one
that I feel will understand me, and will in turn let me peep into
her own life—having confidence in me, that is one the dearest
things between friends, strangers, acquaintances, or kindred."

Pisces live and breathe romance, but they also can prove wary of commitment. In Johnson's case, she seems to have committed to her writing instead of to a mate, generating work so consistently and prolifically that still not all of her writing has been collected.

In 1909, Johnson moved to Vancouver, British Columbia, and not long after she became ill. She died of breast cancer in 1913 at the age of fifty-one.

CASE STUDY #2: W. E. B. DU BOIS

Born in Massachusetts in 1863, W. E. B. Du Bois had a great-grandfather who had been an enslaved person and earned his freedom by fighting in the American Revolution. After attending an integrated school where he stood out as an exceptionally gifted student, Du Bois would go on to earn two bachelor's degrees, one from the historically Black Fisk University and one from Harvard University (which did not accept the credits from Fisk). He then won a scholarship to graduate school and was the first-ever Black man to earn a PhD from Harvard. Although Du Bois had what he described as a relatively happy childhood, he understood the corrosive nature of racism and was moved to directly address its horrors in the service of building a more just society. Throughout his life, Du Bois used his uncontested brilliance to do just that.

Pisces can sometimes cut a rakish figure, but they are often known for their refinement. Du Bois, for example, dressed meticulously, was usually seen wearing pince-nez and carrying a walking stick. He wore an elaborate mustache and goatee and was called Dr. Du Bois by all who knew him.

Pisces can often be so moved by emotion that they are driven to fight, and indeed Du Bois made it his lifelong crusade to fight for racial justice. He cofounded the NAACP and presided over the organization's journal, *The Crisis,* for more than two decades. In the first issue of *The Crisis*, Du Bois wrote, "The object of this publication is to set forth those facts and arguments which show the danger of race prejudice, particularly as manifested today toward colored people. It takes its name from the fact that the editors believe that this is a critical time in the history of the advancement of men." In addition to its political content, *The Crisis* also highlighted Black artists and published some of the most important writers of the time, including Zora Neale Hurston (Capricorn, see page 222), Arna Bontemps (Libra), Gwen-

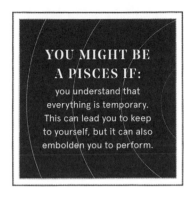

YOU MIGHT BE A PISCES IF:

you understand that everything is temporary. This can lead you to keep to yourself, but it can also embolden you to perform.

dolyn B. Bennett (Cancer), and Countee Cullen (Gemini). It was also the site of Langston Hughes's (Aquarius) first published poem, "The Negro Speaks of Rivers" (1921). Although Du Bois sought to promote Black artistic achievement, his primary purpose with *The Crisis* was always political. Not only were there political articles throughout, but each issue contained a section called "The Lynching Industry" that detailed the names of all the victims of lynchings in the previous year, including the dates and locations, as well as a breakdown of the incidents by race and gender. It is horrifying reading, to put it mildly, but Du Bois knew that in order to enact real change, the crisis must be addressed head-on.

Du Bois was deeply concerned about the health and happiness of African American children who were flooded with constant racist depictions of themselves in the children's books of the day. In response, he created a dedicated children's issue of *The Crisis*, but because he felt it was important not to shield children from the truth of racism while also not traumatizing them, in 1920 he created a separate magazine called *The Brownies' Book,* specifically aimed at Black children. *The Brownies' Book* contained fiction, poetry, games, and articles about current events, as well as letters from readers. He worked on it closely with writer and editor Jessie Redmon Fauset (Taurus, see page 54), and the magazine cemented the importance of creating quality material for Black children and was an early example of a publication that took representation in children's literature into account. Because Pisces is the last sign of the zodiac, it encompasses attributes of all the preceding signs and tends to occupy a space between old age and infancy. As such, Pisces often have a special relationship with children and are able to communicate with them on a level that is at once that of the sage (Aquarius) and of the child (Aries).

Although he was a great supporter of the arts (Pisces almost always are), Du Bois felt strongly that art's purpose absolutely must be political in nature. An intellectual and an activist at heart, he approached literature from the point of view of social reform. He was a proponent of what now might be termed "respectability politics," publishing a controversial essay called "The Criteria for Negro Art" that asserted all art was necessarily propaganda and that this should be taken into consideration by Black artists. This philosophy was unappealing to some of the younger Harlem Renaissance writers like Wallace Thurman (Leo, see page 109), who sought to resist the notion that art should only serve a political end, and who felt that Du Bois's stance was overly conservative.

Although Du Bois's consideration of art stood in contrast to some prominent Harlem Renaissance figures, Du Bois was considered radical, especially in comparison to his political adversary, Booker T. Washington (Aries). Washington argued for an accommodationist philosophy, urging Black people to focus on increasing their financial prosperity, whereas Du Bois proposed a much more proactive response to racism. In a late interview, Du Bois maintained that the differences between them "developed more between our followers than between us." He went on to say, "I never thought Washington was a bad man. I believed him to be sincere, though wrong. He and I came from different backgrounds. I was born free. Washington was born a slave. He felt the lash of an overseer over his back . . . I had a happy childhood and acceptance in the community. Washington's childhood was hard." Ultimately, Du Bois felt that Washington "bartered away much that was not his to barter."

Although Du Bois published five novels, including *The Quest of the Silver Fleece* (1911), *Dark Princess: A Romance* (1928*)*, *The Ordeal of Mansart* (1957), *Mansart Builds a School* (1959), and *Worlds of Color* (1961), it is his nonfiction for which he is most celebrated. He wrote more than two dozen nonfiction books, including *Black Reconstruction in America* (1935), a book that actively refuted the myth that African Americans were responsible for the failures of Reconstruction, as well as an essay collection, *The Souls of Black Folk* (1903), in which he first gave language to the concept of "double consciousness," the idea that Black people in the United States must occupy two identities. He wrote:

It is a peculiar sensation, this double-consciousness, this sense of always looking at one's self through the eyes of others, of measuring one's soul by the tape of a world that looks on in amused contempt and pity. One ever feels his two-ness,—an American, a Negro; two souls, two thoughts, two unreconciled strivings; two warring ideals in one dark body, whose dogged strength alone keeps it from being torn asunder.

The history of the American Negro is the history of strife—this longing to attain self-conscious manhood, to merge his double self into a better and truer self. In the merging he wishes neither of the older selves to be lost.

Du Bois was a private man who seemed to have a stable, quiet personal life. He first married Nina Gormer, with whom he had two children (one died in infancy). After her death, he married the writer Shirley Graham (Scorpio), with whom he stayed until his death. Politics influenced nearly all of his work as he fought for racial justice and social equality at every turn, campaigning as a peace activist, popularizing Pan-Africanism, and supporting women's right to vote, although he was wary of the racism that existed within the movement (see Frances Ellen Watkins Harper, Libra, page 156). In 1951, he was put on trial in the McCarthy hearings under suspicion of anti-American activities. He counted fellow Pisces Albert Einstein among his friends, and Einstein volunteered to serve as a character witness for Du Bois.

Pisces often have an easy time befriending other Pisces— there is a depth of feeling to the sign that is perhaps difficult for other signs to broach.

Because the trial was a clear attempt at character assassination and the charges were ungrounded, they were eventually dropped, but not without taking a toll on Du Bois. At one point in the trial, he was held in chains—as if this eighty-two-year-old man, a paragon of intellectual thought, posed some sort of immediate danger to others in the room. In the aftermath of the trial, he traveled widely, including to China, where he was welcomed and hosted by Mao Zedong (Capricorn). Eventually, he and Shirley settled in Ghana, where he died in 1963 at the age of ninety-three.

CASE STUDY #3: ZITKÁLA-ŠÁ

Like fellow Pisces E. Pauline Johnson, Zitkála-Šá had more than one name. Although she was born Gertrude Simmons and eventually took the married surname Bonnin, Zitkála-Šá was the name she gave herself—a name that means "Red Bird" in the Lakota language. It is fitting that she should have two names. Pisces often exist within a double space, be it in terms of identity, physicality, or spirituality, but for Zitkála-Šá, that double nature was instead a multiplicity manifesting itself in a panoply of talents. She was a teacher, writer, musician, composer, and translator, all while privileging her fight for social equality above all else.

Born on the Yankton Sioux reservation as part of the Ihanktonwan Nation, Zitkála-Šá left home at the age of eight to attend White's Indiana Manual Labor Institute. Ostensibly an educational initiative to help elevate the social position of poor Native children, the school turned out to be a site of extreme trauma for Zitkála-Šá, who was forced to renounce her racial, cultural, and religious identity as well as to cut her hair in an effort to erase any overt ties to her people.

Despite the horrendous living conditions, Zitkála-Šá excelled at the school, and although she left after three years, she eventually returned to concentrate on studying the violin. She earned a scholarship to Earlham College where she succeeded academically, winning several speech contests before being hired to teach at the infamous Carlisle Indian School. Although she seemed to enjoy teaching, she was horrified by the Carlisle School's treatment of its Native students and eventually had a falling-out with the administration. One of the first federally funded boarding schools meant to indoctrinate Native children, the Carlisle Indian School was presided over by Richard Henry Pratt (Sagittarius), a military officer. The noxious quote "kill the Indian to save the man" is attributed to Pratt. In the aftermath of her dispute with Pratt, Zitkála-Šá published an article in the *Atlantic Monthly* decrying the racist, assimilationist mission of the school. Describing her first night at White's Indiana Manual Labor Institute, she writes:

It was night when we reached the school grounds. The lights from the windows of the large buildings fell upon some of the icicled trees that stood beneath them. We were led toward an open door, where the brightness of the lights within flooded out over the heads of the excited palefaces who blocked the way. My body trembled more from fear than from the snow I trod upon.

She goes on to describe a situation in which she is treated as a plaything at best and neglected at worst. When she cries, one of the older children whispers, "Wait until you are alone in the night." To which she responds, "Oh, I want my mother and my brother Dawée! I want to go to my aunt!" That night in bed, she considers her situation:

> I had arrived in the wonderful land of rosy skies, but I was not happy, as I had thought I should be. My long travel and the bewildering sights had exhausted me. I fell asleep, heaving deep, tired sobs. My tears were left to dry themselves in streaks, because neither my aunt nor my mother was near to wipe them away.

The school's response was to criticize her for speaking out against the institution from which, according to them, she had benefited so greatly. Zitkála-Šá continued to publish essays in the *Atlantic Monthly*, including an essay called "Why I Am a Pagan" (1902), which proclaimed both her love for the natural world and her conviction that the natural and spiritual world were intrinsically connected. The essay concludes:

> A wee child toddling in a wonder world, I prefer to their dogma my excursions into the natural gardens where the voice of the Great Spirit is heard in the twittering of the birds, the rippling of mighty waters, and the sweet breathing of flowers. If this is Paganism, then at present, at least, I am a Pagan.

This was audacious for anyone to publish in the *Atlantic Monthly* at the turn of the twentieth century, let alone a woman of color. Pisces have a tendency to push against the status quo when you least expect it.

A tremendously talented musician, Zitkála-Šá trained at the New England Conservatory of Music and even played for President McKinley at the White House in 1900. That prodigious talent would lead her to write the music and the libretto for the first-ever Native American opera, *The Sun Dance* (1913), which was staged in collaboration with Brigham Young professor William F. Hanson.

The Sun Dance was a celebration of Native culture and an attempt to preserve sacred dance and songs, all presented in a form that white American culture could understand. With a mixed Native and non-Native cast, *The Sun Dance* played throughout Utah and would eventually go on to premiere in New York City just after Zitkála-Šá's death in 1938.

Something of a historian and folklorist, Zitkála-Šá collected stories not only from her own people but from a variety of different tribes, which she then translated into English and Latin. Her collections, *Old Indian Legends* (1901) and *American Indian Stories* (1921), were some of the earliest collections of Native work by a Native person.

In 1902, she married Raymond Talephause Bonnin (Gemini), a man from her tribe who became a war hero. Together they raised a son while working for the Bureau of Indian Affairs. Eventually they moved to Washington, DC, and from that point on, Zitkála-Šá devoted her life to Indian rights. She was the secretary of the Society of American Indians and played a pivotal role in the Indian Citizenship Act of 1924. Together with her husband, she created the National Council of American Indians, of which she served as president, and she created the Indian Welfare Committee. She died in 1938 and, along with her husband, is buried in Arlington National Cemetery.

CODA: ARTHUR MACHEN

Pisces are often seen as the mystics of the zodiac, and in Arthur Machen, that mysticism comes to the fore. Born in Wales to an Anglican preacher and his wife, Machen evinced an early love for literature, proving a voracious reader who from the outset showed an interest in the occult.

As an adult, Machen worked as a journalist, a tutor, and an actor, but it is as a writer and occultist that his true Piscean nature can be observed. Although he had always been cognizant of a spiritual realm and saw no problem in combining his interest in the unseen world with his rather conservative religious views, it was the untimely death of his wife, Amelia, that catalyzed Machen's deeper exploration of the occult. In the aftermath of her death, he found his sanity challenged, and he experienced a series of what could only be described as paranormal events. He was good friends with A. E. Waite (Libra), who along with Pamela Coleman Smith (Aquarius) created the classic Rider-Waite-Smith Tarot. Through this friendship, Machen's enthusiasm for mysticism and ritual grew, even joining the Hermetic Order of the Golden Dawn for a short while.

Whatever occult experiences Machen may have had, they clearly informed his fiction, which walks a line between the fantastical and the horrifying, ultimately landing on the weird, a genre to which he would give birth. With strange tales such as *The Hill of Dreams* (1907) and "The White People" (1904), he took readers on psychedelic journeys into the heart of the unknown.

In perhaps his most famous work, *The Great God Pan* (1890), Machen tells a bizarre story of medical experimentation gone terribly wrong. A young woman is subjected to brain surgery in the hope that it might render her able to perceive unseen realms. The gruesome procedure culminates in her coming face to face with the great god, Pan. The woman not only goes mad, but the surgery prompts unexpected consequences that span generations, with her progeny becoming infected by the horrific knowledge of what lies beyond this existence.

To some degree, all Pisces are cognizant of the veil between the worlds. Some do not dare to look beyond it. Some take a peek now and again, and some Pisces—like Machen—are capable of walking right through to the other side.

NOTES FOR WRITERS WITH OTHER PISCES PLACEMENTS

WRITER'S CORNER

POSITIVE ASPECTS

You are multitalented and capable of tapping into your creative nature more than probably any other sign.

NEGATIVE ASPECTS

You can get distracted easily and can sometimes be lazy. Make sure not to let yourself off the hook too easily.

WRITER BEWARE

You have a tendency to wander toward illusion. Make sure to set concrete goals for yourself so you stay on task.

PISCES MOON: You see the good in everyone and are not shy about expressing your affection. You can be driven by a beautiful kind of idealism that will make your writing shine. As a very sensitive person, make sure you give yourself a writing space that makes you feel safe and focused. Because your emotions are ruled by a mutable sign, that writing space may need to change frequently.

PISCES RISING: You often embody the most overt aspects of the sign in a way that is visible to others. You are naturally vivacious, and others are easily drawn to your friendliness and warmth. Because you are a performer, you may be drawn to the theater and might even consider writing a one-person show. Your bugbears are a tendency to be disorganized and a sense of pessimism. Stay positive, trust yourself, clean up your desk, and you should be good to go.

MERCURY IN PISCES: You may be a born poet. Your natural intuition is so strong it borders on the psychic, and as such, you have access to artistic wells that not everyone else has. Your words can create worlds.

VENUS IN PISCES: You have a naturally romantic flair that gives your work that certain je ne sais quoi that all writers wish they had. When preparing to write, you would do well to dress in something that makes you feel in touch with the etheric realms. Perhaps bell sleeves or an ascot?

MARS IN PISCES: You have access to a deep, roiling well of passion and the ability to transmute that into meaningful art. This is the placement of the artist who is able to make something concrete of all those ineffable emotions that a different sign may barely be able to identify. Your own downfall may be poor boundaries. If you find that you keep missing writing time because of someone else's needs, try to be more vigilant about carving out artistic space for yourself.

TRY THIS!

+ SET your alarm for the middle of the night. Write a poem while you're still half-asleep.

+ GO on a treasure hunt in nature. Make a list of found objects you must collect. Use them as inspiration for a story.

+ LISTEN to a genre of music you don't normally listen to. Freewrite and see where it takes you.

READER'S CORNER:

COMPATIBILITY CHART

Which Pisces-composed book is most likely to appeal to you? It depends on your sign. Look for your match below. And don't forget to look at your rising and Moon signs if you know those.

SIGN	CLASSIC	MODERN
ARIES	E. PAULINE JOHNSON, *The White Wampum*	GABRIEL GARCÍA MÁRQUEZ, *One Hundred Years of Solitude*
TAURUS	STÉPHANE MALLARMÉ, *Poésies*	DENNIS J. SWEENEY, *In the Antarctic Circle*
GEMINI	ALGERNON BLACKWOOD, *The Willows*	LESLIE MARMON SILKO, *Almanac of the Dead*
CANCER	ZITKÁLA-ŠÁ, *Old Indian Legends*	NOVA REN SUMA, *17 & Gone*
LEO	HENRY WADSWORTH LONGFELLOW, *Hyperion: A Romance*	DAVE EGGERS, *A Heartbreaking Work of Staggering Genius*
VIRGO	VICTOR HUGO, *Les Misérables*	EMILY ST. JOHN MANDEL, *The Glass Hotel*
LIBRA	W. E. B. DU BOIS, *Black Reconstruction in America*	SUSANNAH NEVISON, *Lethal Theater*

SIGN	CLASSIC	MODERN
SCORPIO	**EDWARD GOREY,** *The Doubtful Guest*	**APRIL GENEVIEVE TUCHOLKE,** *The Boneless Mercies*
SAGITTARIUS	**EDNA ST. VINCENT MILLAY,** *The King's Henchman*	**JACK KEROUAC,** *On the Road*
CAPRICORN	**ELIZABETH BARRETT BROWNING,** *The Seraphim, and Other Poems*	**WILLIAM GIBSON,** *Neuromancer*
AQUARIUS	**WILLIAM GODWIN,** *Enquiry Concerning Political Justice, and Its Influence on General Virtue and Happiness*	**DOUGLAS ADAMS,** *The Hitchhiker's Guide to the Galaxy*
PISCES	**W. H. AUDEN,** *City Without Walls and Other Poems*	**DAVID FOSTER WALLACE,** *Infinite Jest*

A NOTE ON CUSP FIGURES

CUSPS ARE THE IMAGINARY LINES BETWEEN HOUSES.

Authors born near the transition from one astrological season to the next can embody qualities of both signs in a way that makes them a bit difficult to pin down. Take, for example, the infamous Lord Byron (born January 22, 1778), an Aquarius born on the Capricorn-Aquarius cusp. In 1809, Byron set out on a tour of the Mediterranean. Along the way he began his poetic travelogue, which would later be called *Childe Harold's Pilgrimage*. The poem is essentially the nineteenth-century poetry version of a Wes Anderson movie—in it, a moody antihero takes in the beauties of the world, then passes them by. Later, when Byron published the first cantos of the work, the initial print run sold out in three days, catapulting Byron to literary celebrity. Women threw themselves at his feet—including Lady Caroline Lamb (Scorpio), the tempestuous lover who deemed him "mad—bad—and dangerous to know." Byron had a bevy of lovers, including women, men, and even his half-sister. He got married; sired the future mathematician Ada Lovelace (Sagittarius); separated from his wife; and struck up an affair with Mary Shelley's (Virgo, see page 131) stepsister, Claire Clairmont (Taurus). Byron spent time with the Shelleys on the shores of Lake Geneva, and was present for the inception of both *Frankenstein* and *The Vampyre*, which was at least based on a fragment of his work, if not on his person (it was totally based on his person). In 1823, deciding he hadn't done enough to help humankind, Byron became involved in the Greek War of Independence; he was proclaimed a national hero following his death.

For all the contradictions he embodied, Byron was nothing if not self-aware. His comedic masterpiece *Don Juan* (pronounced "Joo-an" for the sake of easy, funny rhymes) turns the Don Juan archetype on its head, presenting a hero who, rather than acting like a total Lothario, simply can't help but attract those around him and is easily seduced. The poem contains some sick burns, too—for example, Don Juan's mother loves mathematics, and Byron calls her a "walking calculation." (He'd once referred to his ex as his "Princess of Parallelograms.") The poem includes topics ranging from sexual exploits to cannibalism to piracy to war, and is inflected by a sort of stylish, satirical detachment.

How do you sum up a literary figure like that? "Talented poet" is accurate but feels insufficient. Idealist, lover of freedom, and selfless participant in other people's war ? These skirt the scandals. And alongside the scandals, there was plenty of cruelty—for example, Byron eventually claimed custody of his child with Claire Clairmont and that child died in a convent, perhaps for want of her heartbroken mother's care and affection.

The point of this exercise is to highlight how taking cusps into account can be helpful when endeavoring to understand unknowns surrounding slippery literary figures. Perhaps in the excess and damage surrounding Byron we see the products of an inability to balance his dueling natures. Or perhaps we see the clash of Aquarian ideals with Capricorn mystery.

READING LIST:

Books Written by Cusp Figures

PASQUIN by Henry Fielding (Aries–Taurus cusp)

GOODNIGHT MOON by Margaret Wise Brown (Taurus–Gemini cusp)

SELECTED POEMS by Anna Laetitia Barbauld (Gemini–Cancer cusp)

SELECTED POEMS by Hart Crane (Cancer–Leo cusp)

IN A GLASS DARKLY by J. Sheridan Le Fanu (Leo–Virgo cusp)

THE TIME MACHINE by H. G. Wells (Virgo–Libra cusp)

THE GOLDEN NOTEBOOK by Doris Lessing (Libra–Scorpio cusp)

SILAS MARNER by George Eliot (Scorpio–Sagittarius cusp)

OUR LADY OF THE FLOWERS by Jean Genet (Sagittarius–Capricorn cusp)

DON JUAN by Lord Byron (Capricorn–Aquarius cusp)

THE DIARY OF OTHERS by Anaïs Nin (Aquarius–Pisces cusp)

SOME FINAL THOUGHTS

We hope that you've found something here for you, even if you don't conform to the most dominant astrological types...

Whether you're the Aries who doesn't like conflict

Or the Taurus as flexible as a paperback spine

Whether you're the shyest Gemini at the party

Or the Cancer who dances on tables

Whether you're the Leo reading books in the library alcove

Or the Virgo in need of some chaos

Whether you're the Libra who can always decide

Or the Scorpio with the softest of hearts

Whether you're the Sagittarius who stays home reading Kant

Or the Capricorn who stays up reading King

Whether you're the Aquarius who delights in romance

Or the Pisces too practical for poetry

We hope you'll use astrology like we hope you'll use literature—to empower you, to open your mind to unseen wonders, and your heart to untold joys.

To paraphrase Walt Whitman, remember that people—all people—contain multitudes.

ACKNOWLEDGMENTS

The greatest of thanks to our amazing editor, Sara Neville, and to all the people at Clarkson Potter who helped this book come into being: Julie Ehlers, Ashley Pierce, Lise Sukhu, Danielle Deschenes, Kelli Tokos, and Chloe Aryeh. Thanks to our fabulous agents, Becky LeJeune and Anne Tibbets.

Thank you to astrologer extraordinaire Adam Elenbaas, and to Michelle Corbesier and Delia Gallegos for teaching us astrology. To Chani Nicholas and Nadiya Shah who don't know us, but who helped anyway. To Stephanie Insley Hershinow, Anne C. McCarthy, and Rebecca Ariel Porte, who helped us understand Austen and Wollstonecraft and Keats, and to Zeeshan Reshamwala, who shared his expertise on Henry Derozio. To Quill Camp, who read drafts; Camille DeAngelis, who helped think things through; and to Kristen Kittscher, who not only helped with the astrology, but who also kept this book on track in every possible way.

And thanks to those whose support has fueled us along the path: the late Keith Abbott, Mona Awad, duncan b. barlow, Julia Michie Bruckner, James Camp, Jocelyn Camp, Phoebe Camp, Julie Caplan, Dave Cass, Rebecca Colesworthy, Nan Z. Da, Noël Da, Sarah Ehlers, Andrea Feder, Jed Feder, Rob Feder, Leslie Good, Anupriya Gruber, Joel Gruber, Monira Gruber, Sam Hansen, Patricia Hernandez, Erin Hittesdorf, Amy Keys, Brian Kiteley, Moshe Kornfeld, Nathaniel Kornfeld, Noah Kornfeld, the Kornfeld Krewe, Brian Laidlaw, Marjorie Levinson, Chet Lisiecki, Suzanne Motley, Alicia Mountain, Thirii Myo Kyaw Myint, Emily Pettit, Michelle Naka Pierce, Esther Shaffer Plassmeyer, Khadijah Queen, Dylan Rice-Leary, Ezra Rich, Sara Rich, Kyra Riddell, Natalie Rogers, Maya Shaffer, Sierra Shaffer, Isak Sjursen, Sasha Tamar Strelitz, Dennis J. Sweeney, Clayton Szczech, Sheera Talpaz, Tiffany Tatreau, Kathi Templeman, Ted Templeman, Alison Turner, and Andrew Wille.

ABOUT THE AUTHORS

McCORMICK TEMPLEMAN is the author of the novels *The Little Woods* and *The Glass Casket*. A graduate of Reed College, she holds an MFA in creative writing from Naropa University and a PhD in English with a creative writing emphasis from the University of Denver. She also holds a master's degree and a second doctorate in the field of Traditional Chinese Medicine. She teaches at Sweet Briar College and serves as the fiction editor at Astrophil Press.

RACHEL FEDER is an associate professor of English and literary arts at the University of Denver and the author of the nonfiction books *Harvester of Hearts: Motherhood Under the Sign of Frankenstein* and *The Darcy Myth: Jane Austen, Literary Heartthrobs, and the Monsters They Taught Us to Love*. She is also the author of *Birth Chart*, a collection of poems about astrology, motherhood, and literary history.

INDEX

Copyright © 2023 by Rachel Feder and McCormick Templeman

Illustrations copyright © 2023 by Mike Willcox
Illustration colorist: Lise Sukhu

Published in the United States by Clarkson Potter/Publishers,
an imprint of the Crown Publishing Group, a division of Penguin
Random House LLC, New York.

clarksonpotter.com

CLARKSON POTTER is a trademark and POTTER with colophon
is a registered trademark of Penguin Random House LLC.

Library of Congress Control Number: 2023939232

ISBN 978-0-593-57973-2
Ebook ISBN 978-0-593-57974-9

Printed in China

Editor: Sara Neville
Production Editor: Ashley Pierce
Designer: Lise Sukhu
Production Manager: Kelli Tokos
Book and cover design by: Lise Sukhu
Copy Editor: Julie Ehlers
Proofreaders: Elisabeth Beller and Michael Fedison
Indexer: Ken DellaPenta
Marketer: Chloe Aryeh

10 9 8 7 6 5 4 3 2 1

First Edition